PREVENTING SUBSTANCE ABUSE AMONG CHILDREN AND ADOLESCENTS

Pergamon Titles of Related Interest

Ellis/McInerney/DiGiuseppe/Yeager RATIONAL-EMOTIVE THERAPY
WITH ALCOHOLICS AND SUBSTANCE ABUSERS
Hester/Miller HANDBOOK OF ALCOHOLISM TREATMENT
APPROACHES: AN INTEGRATIVE APPROACH
Knott ALCOHOL PROBLEMS

Related Journals *

CLINICAL PSYCHOLOGY REVIEW
JOURNAL OF CHILD PSYCHOLOGY AND PSYCHIATRY
AND APPLIED DISCIPLINES
JOURNAL OF SUBSTANCE ABUSE TREATMENT

*Free sample copies available upon request

PSYCHOLOGY PRACTITIONER GUIDEBOOKS

EDITORS

Arnold P. Goldstein, Syracuse University
Leonard Krasner, Stanford University & SUNY at Stony Brook
Sol L. Garfield, Washington University in St. Louis

PREVENTING SUBSTANCE ABUSE AMONG CHILDREN AND ADOLESCENTS

JEAN E. RHODES
LEONARD A. JASON
DePaul University

PERGAMON PRESS
New York · Oxford · Beijing · Frankfurt
São Paulo · Sydney · Tokyo · Toronto

U.S.A.	Pergamon Press, Inc., Maxwell House, Fairview Park, Elmsford, New York 10523, U.S.A.
U.K.	Pergamon Press plc, Headington Hill Hall, Oxford OX3 0BW, England
PEOPLE'S REPUBLIC OF CHINA	Pergamon Press, Room 4037, Qianmen Hotel, Beijing, People's Republic of China
FEDERAL REPUBLIC OF GERMANY	Pergamon Press GmbH, Hammerweg 6, D-6242 Kronberg, Federal Republic of Germany
BRAZIL	Pergamon Editora Ltda, Rua Eça de Queiros, 346, CEP 04011, Paraiso, São Paulo, Brazil
AUSTRALIA	Pergamon Press Australia Pty Ltd., P.O. Box 544, Ports Point, N.S.W. 2011, Australia
JAPAN	Pergamon Press, 5th Floor, Matsuoka Central Building, 1-7-1 Nishishinjuku, Shinjuku-ku, Tokyo 160, Japan
CANADA	Pergamon Press Canada Ltd., Suite No. 271, 253 College Street, Toronto, Ontario, Canada M5T 1R5

Copyright © 1988 Pergamon Books, Inc.

All Rights Reserved. No part of this publication may be reproduced, stored in a retrieval system or transmitted in any form or by any means: electronic, electrostatic, magnetic tape, mechanical, photocopying, recording or otherwise, without permission in writing from the publishers.

First edition 1988

Library of Congress Cataloging in Publication Data
Rhodes, Jean E.
Preventing substance abuse among children and adolescents.
(Psychology practitioner guidebooks)
Bibliography: p.
Includes indexes.
1. Youth — United States — Substance use. 2. Children — United States — Substances use. 3. Substance abuse — United States — Prevention. I. Jason, Leonard. II. Title. III. Series.
[DNLM: 1. Substance Abuse — in adolescence. 2. Substance Abuse — in infancy & childhood. 3. Substance Abuse — prevention & control. WM 270 R476p]
HV4999.Y68R46   1988   362.2'9   87-32885

British Library Cataloguing in Publication Data
Rhodes, Jean E.
Preventing substance abuse among children and adolescents.
— (Psychology practitioner guidebooks).
1. Youth — Alcohol use. 2. Youth — Drug use.
I. Title. II. Jason, Leonard A. III. Series.
362.2'9'088054   HV5135

ISBN 0-08-035753-9 Hard cover
ISBN 0-08-035752-0 Flexicover

Printed in Great Britain by A. Wheaton & Co. Ltd., Exeter

Contents

List of Figures

List of Tables

Preface

A photograph of an assortment of drugs recently appeared in the *New York Times,* accompanied by the caption "Do you know what your child is taking in school this year?" The message urged adults to become more involved in preventing youthful substance abuse, and to seek the assistance of practitioners in prevention. This is an example of how our nation's efforts to curb the alarming levels of substance abuse among children and adolescents have heightened in recent years. Unfortunately, despite the generous budgetary allocations and the remarkable media campaign that has characterized recent anti-drug efforts, there are no easy solutions to the problem. Substance abuse among youth remains a complex problem that presents a significant challenge to mental health practitioners. Meeting this challenge will involve incorporating our current knowledge concerning the development of adolescent substance abuse into comprehensive primary prevention strategies.

The object of this book is to provide practitioners with a developmental framework for a better understanding of the factors contributing to substance abuse, and to critique the campaigns, curricula, and related efforts designed to prevent substance abuse among children and adolescents. This understanding should facilitate practitioners' abilities to meet the growing demand for consultation and assistance in the field of substance abuse prevention.

To achieve this objective, the book has been organized into six chapters. Chapter 1 provides a review of studies dealing with the prevalence and consequences of drug use and abuse among our nation's youth. We noted that substance use is widespread in the United States, with nearly all 12th grade students reporting alcohol use (92%) and nearly two-thirds reporting the use of cigarettes (69%) and illicit drugs (61%). We discussed some of the challenges of childhood and adolescence and the ways in which problematic drug use and other risk-taking behaviors can develop.

In Chapter 2, we review the major theories that have been advanced to explain and predict substance abuse. We suggest that the heavy emphasis placed on individual factors by these models limits their ability to provide comprehensive explanations of the antecedents and correlates of substance abuse. We present the social stress model as an alternative approach to the study of adolescent substance abuse. This model integrates the emphasis on individual and systemic variables with recent research on competence and coping. Additionally, in contrast to most theoretical approaches, the social stress model seeks to explicitly address the broader social variables that influence adolescent behavior.

In Chapter 3, we present an overview of the existing prevention strategies, ranging from drug education and behavioral skills training to more community-based approaches. The theoretical base and effectiveness of programs using these approaches was reviewed. In our analysis of these programs, we interpret the findings from a theoretical position that integrated many of the developmental, stress, and ecological concepts that were introduced in the earlier chapters.

Chapter 4 focuses on issues relating to the identification and treatment of at-risk youth. Whereas the primary prevention programs reviewed in Chapter 3 are appropriate for most youth, it may be necessary to provide more intensive and differentiated interventions for youth at higher risk for developing chronic patterns of substance abuse. We present a "multiple gating" early identification procedure, and a set of guidelines for referring these high-risk youths to appropriate treatment services.

In Chapter 5, we present practical guidelines and a process for translating the theory and strategies reviewed in the earlier chapters into effective action. We discuss issues related to entering an agency or school system and determining appropriate goals and objectives. A detailed skills-based curricula, YOUTH SKILLS, is presented as an approach that can be adapted to substance abuse prevention classes and community-based programs. All of the materials to complete each activity, including step-by-step instructions, are provided in the text and appendices. These appendixes also provide an annotated index to available substance abuse prevention resources, including: organizations, relevant publications, "packaged" skills-based curricula, and available funding sources. Finally, we provide guidelines and instruments with which to conduct evaluations of substance abuse prevention programs.

In Chapter 6, we provide an overview and discuss some of the future trends that may be emerging in the field of substance abuse prevention. We conclude that comprehensive substance abuse strategies, as described in this book, offer the most promise, as we address the challenge: to prevent substance abuse among children and adolescents.

Acknowledgements

There are a number of people to whom we would like to express our deepest thanks. We appreciate the continued support and encouragement provided by Linda Hargnett and the staff at the Illinois Addictions Research Institute. We are indebted to Nancy G. Rhodes and Interleaf, Inc. for developing the tables and graphs that appear in this book. We wish to thank George W. Albee, Robert D. Felner, Midge Wilson, Mort M. Silverman, Mary Ann Pentz, William T. Atkins, Patrick H. Tolan, Jean Ann Linney, Matthew Selekman, Janice Freeman, and Cheryl Lonak for their willingness to review earlier drafts and provide thoughtful feedback. We appreciate the production support provided by Pergamon Press, particularly Jerry Frank and Mary Grace Luke. Finally, we would like to thank our families and friends for their encouragement and patience throughout the preparation of this book.

Chapter 1

Introduction

Walking by an elementary school with a large playground, we recently observed a group of children during recess. The array of social interactions among the children was remarkable. For example, some children seemed to be rather popular and played cooperatively with each other, whereas others appeared less adept in their interactions. One child was rejected by the other children when he attempted to aggressively enter their group. Another child was sulking as she played alone in a sand box. We also saw a group of children exerting pressure on a peer to climb a very tall tree. On the street next to the playground, we noticed several adolescents, all of whom were smoking cigarettes.

During just a few minutes of casual observation, we had noticed a few of the numerous social interactions among these children. Which of these interactions represents an orientation that could predispose the children to later problem behaviors, such as drug abuse? Only within a developmental framework can these observations be placed into a theoretical and conceptual web from which we might better understand the meaning of these behaviors, how they come to represent risk factors, and ultimately, what we can do to help these youngsters. But before undertaking an analysis of these developmental factors, we will review the extent of the drug experimentation and abuse problem among children and adolescents.

EXTENT OF THE PROBLEM

Even at the elementary school age, children are experimenting with substances. By substances, we are referring to tobacco, alcohol and illegal drugs such as marijuana, cocaine, LSD and amphetamines. One out of every six children will use marijuana by the seventh grade, and for some this early experimentation leads to regular use. It is estimated that by the time children have reached the twelfth grade, 91% of them will have tried alcohol, 68% will have tried cigarettes, and 61% will have tried an illegal substance (Johnston, O'Malley, & Bachman, 1986). By the senior year, 45% of the boys and 28% of the girls will be drinking

1

heavily (i.e., five or more drinks in a row) during any given two week time period. About 5% of these students will be either drinking alcohol or using marijuana on a daily basis. This is probably an underestimation of the extent of the problem, as many of the students who experience school failure will have dropped out of school by the senior year and are not even included in these statistics. Dropout rates in urban inner-city schools approach 50%, and many dropout incidents are in some ways caused by, related to, or influenced by substance abuse (Friedman, 1985a).

Substance abuse is a major contributor to motor vehicle accidents, medical problems, and other risk-related behaviors in youth. Violent deaths, including accidents, homicides, and suicides, account for more than 77% of mortalities among 15- to 24-year-olds, and substance use is the strongest thread tying these casualties together (Harris, 1985). Motor vehicle accidents account for two-thirds of the total number of these violent deaths, and many of these young victims were driving while under the influence of drugs. Each year, about five thousand youth are homicide victims, and another five thousand commit suicide (Holinger, 1987); many of these deaths are associated with drug abuse. While the personal losses to the affected youth and their families are enormous, the financial cost to society is also large in terms of lost productivity, medical expenses, and crime. For example, substance abuse cost taxpayers approximately $205 billion dollars in fiscal year 1986 alone (Kumpfer, 1987).

IDENTIFYING RISK FACTORS

To better understand why these devastating outcomes occur and to begin the process of developing preventive interventions, we need to identify the childhood and adolescent risk factors associated with substance abuse. Some available evidence suggests that children who are socially incompetent and aggressive are at a greater risk of developing later drug problems than those who are more popular. A number of studies have shown that antisocial behaviors, such as aggressiveness, can predict — as early as the first grade — early initiation and later substance abuse (Spivack, 1983; Kellam & Brown, 1982). In addition, use of drugs in early childhood is strongly correlated with later involvement with more dangerous drugs and an increased probability of problem behavior, including selling drugs and other crimes (Robins & Przybeck, 1985). But why is it that these patterns of aggressiveness have such long-term negative influences on children? Children who are inappropriately aggressive quickly develop reputations as being difficult, and many become increasingly isolated and rejected (Coie & Dodge, 1983). Some of these youngsters have — or soon develop — academic problems as well. If they have not developed positive relationships with their peer groups or their teachers, and have repeatedly experienced failure and the consequent loss of self-esteem, at-risk behaviors such as drug experimentation might represent attempts to escape or deny current life difficulties, or to flaunt family and school expectations and regulations. For others, drug experimentation might represent the only way to earn approval from others who are actively experimenting with drugs. Of course, these explanations are only a few of the possible pathways through which we can understand how children begin to experiment with drugs. Let's now look more closely at some of the developmental issues confronting children and adolescents, and how these issues can place youngsters at risk for engaging in a variety of risky behaviors.

The developmental issues will be examined with a consideration of the transactional model offered by Sameroff and Chandler (1975). From this perspective, the development of the child is the product of the dynamic interaction of the child and the experience provided by his or her family and social context. Substance abuse and other problem behaviors can be understood as the result of a "synergistic transaction" between individual constitutional factors impacting on environmental conditions, which in turn affect the individual, who then influences the environment (Sameroff & Chandler, 1975). Sameroff (1987) offers the following scenario to illustrate this complex interplay of the child and environment over time:

> A complicated childbirth may make an otherwise calm mother somewhat anxious. The mother's anxiety during the first months of the child's life may cause her to be uncertain and inappropriate in her interactions with the child. In response to such inconsistency, the infant may develop some irregularities in feeding and sleeping patterns that give the appearance of a difficult temperament. This difficult temperament decreases the pleasure that the mother obtains from the child, so she tends to spend less time with the child. If no adult interacts with the child, the child may not meet the norms for language development and score poorly on preschool language tests. In this case, the outcome was not determined by the complicated birth nor by the mother's consequent emotional response. (p. 76)

This transactional framework can be extended through childhood and adolescence to better understand the development of substance abuse and other problem behaviors. For example, the child who performs poorly on the preschool tests may feel less confident as a student, leading to difficult interactions with teachers and peers. These difficulties may further exacerbate the child's lack of comfort in social situations, and he or she may seek out other individuals in similar situations. Thus, a series of transactional patterns can spiral toward the child engaging in problem behaviors.

In the following chapters, we will be considering this transactional perspective as it relates to the risk for substance abuse. The potential contribution of biological factors such as the genetic contribution of parents, the pre-natal environment and physiological/cognitive disorders are considered to be constitutional vulnerabilities that are either exacerbated or mitigated by the stressors, attachments, coping skills and resources in the youth's environment. See Kumpfer (1987) for an excellent overview of these biological risk factors.

Early Childhood Factors

We can see factors in early childhood (roughly 1.5 to 6 years of age) that may predispose a child toward later behavioral difficulties and drug abuse. The characteristic ways of relating to others become pronounced and relatively stable in early childhood, and these enduring patterns can influence later interpersonal relations. As children begin to experiment with independence and autonomy from their parents (Erikson, 1959), they begin to explore new settings, learn new games, and form new relationships with peers. Peer groups help children form attitudes and values, and provide a forum for the child to begin to challenge parental values. These peer relations have important implications for later adjustment, because it is within this context that children learn to successfully cooperate and compete with each other and to deal with aggression (Hartup, 1979). In other words, children are learning to become socially competent, equipped with numerous subtle and not-so-subtle verbal and nonverbal tactics for maneuvering in the complex social arena. To the extent that children have developed a good repertoire of these social competencies, they are better able to relate to and gain support from their peer groups. In addition, the availability of a supportive peer network can serve as a buffer that can offset the influence of stressors (Cohen & Adler, 1986). Those who are socially isolated and rejected are at a disadvantage and are at greater risk for developing later difficulties (Coie & Dodge, 1983; Cowen, Pederson, Babigian, Izzo, & Trost, 1973).

Late Childhood Factors

During late childhood (roughly ages 6 to 11), parents continue to play a key role. Even though the child spends an increasing amount of time with peers, the family is still the most important influence during later childhood. The family transmits values and standards, and if there is an atmosphere of love, support, and respect, there is a greater chance that these family norms will be incorporated into the emerging value system of the children. The success of this identification will be an important factor in healthy adjustment during adolescence.

The self-concept is established during late childhood (Erikson, 1959). It is a reflection of a child's confidence in his or her ability to cope with obstacles and solve problems successfully. Because children's self-concepts are influenced by their past experiences with problem solving and interaction, those who are less confident in their ability to successfully cope with difficulties may be at risk for later maladaptive coping behaviors. Those with an inadequately developed self-concept might be more influenced by peer groups because their own esteem can only be stabilized or fortified by attention from others. If such peer groups tend to experiment with drugs, a child is more likely to join in these efforts than to risk peer rejection and the resulting lowered self-esteem.

Adolescent Factors

Adolescence (roughly ages 11 to 19) is a turbulent stage where major changes are occurring in physical, intellectual, and moral processes. It is a time when youth are most at risk for experimenting with substances and developing patterns of abuse. It is a time of identity formation, a process both painful and growth-enhancing. For the adolescent, the imperfection of the world becomes a salient issue (Baumrind, 1985). Gradually, adolescents begin to question their parents' absolute authority as well as certain social conventions (e.g., dress codes). In giving up a view of parental authority as absolute, adolescents also reject certain parental standards (e.g., disapproval of all drugs), and this can lead to experimentation with substances (Turiel, 1978).

At the same time that adolescents begin to question certain parental standards, the peer group becomes increasingly significant. The adolescents' peers take on a larger role in transmitting values and standards. Most adolescents, even those who are relatively independent, will conform with peer standards to achieve status and identity within the peer group (Jessor & Jessor, 1977). If one's peers are experimenting with illegal substances and peer approval is critical, then the child can face the dilemma of either abstaining, thus damaging friendships and facing possible isolation, or joining with peers in experimentation, thus creating further alienation from parental standards.

Adolescence is also characterized by a heightened concern with appearance, personal qualities, and abilities (Elkind, 1978), and a decrease in self-esteem. Low self-esteem coincides with puberty-induced physical changes, and the transition into the larger, often more threatening junior high school. The adolescents' reduced self-esteem is painful, in part, because they lack the perspective to realize that their suffering is developmentally normative and usually temporary (Baumrind, 1985).

At this stage, many learn how to manage and tolerate emotional pain, but for some the process is too painful and they escape into the safety of regressive behavior patterns (e.g., excessive dependency, anorexia, isolation). Alarmingly high suicide rates and health compromising behaviors are, in part, reflections of the depth and extent of suffering that youth experience during this period.

Developmental Factors and Substance Abuse. This brief sketch of the developmental issues illustrates how the changes during this period can increase the adolescent's risk of yielding to various direct and indirect pressures to experiment with drugs. The combination of increased self-consciousness, lowered self-esteem, and increased reliance on the peer group can promote substance use in those youngsters who are rejecting parental standards. This is a time when adolescents discover inconsistencies in adults' arguments concerning the potential risks of substance use, particularly given the fact that many parents drink alcoholic beverages and smoke cigarettes. Is it possible to reverse these potent behavior influences on youngsters, in order to decrease their risk of adopting health compromising behaviors? Perhaps preventive programs with a keen appreciation of the role of risk-taking in adolescent development, particularly in maintaining peer relationships, will have a greater chance of gaining adolescents' trust and cooperation and developing appropriate preventive programs. A developmental perspective should also enable practitioners to discern between developmentally normal adolescent risk-taking and substance use, and the more serious patterns of problem behavior and substsance abuse.

Of course the key question is: Why do some children experience the challenges of adolescence as opportunities for growth and independence, while others attempt to cope with these issues through substance abuse? Epidemiological research has suggested that a range of family, school, and social variables may place certain youth at greater risk for substance abuse. The identification of these risk factors has enabled researchers to better predict which adolescents may develop patterns of problem behavior.

One of the most important predictors of problem behavior is parental family management techniques. In their drive toward independence, adolescents will typically question the basis of their parents' standards. Some parents are sensitive to these developmental shifts, negotiating limits while encouraging independence; others may be more punitive, rejecting, and excessively harsh. These factors can influence the youth's decision to use drugs (Baumrind, 1985) (Kumpher, 1987). In addition, parental criminology, substance abuse, antisocial behavior, and inconsistency are predictors of youthful substance abuse. Children who live in homes with inconsistent and ineffective family management practices are less likely to identify with their parents and incorporate their values and standards. Youngsters from such homes are more likely to associate with others who are experiencing similar difficult home lives, and these peers may influence each other to experiment with drugs.

One of the strongest predictors of substance use is the adolescent's peer-dominated social network (Jessor, Chase, & Donovan, 1980). After age and sex, the factor most likely to be common among a youngster's peer group is drug use (Kandel, Kessler, & Margulies, 1978). This suggests that youth may actually select peers with a similar level of substance use. Those who select friends who do not experiment with drugs have probably developed positive relationships with their parents. Strong identification with parental standards against drug abuse will decrease the likelihood that these youth will develop attachments to drug-abusing peers in early adolescence, because the behaviors rewarded in the family and those likely to be rewarded by such peers are not compatible (Hawkins, Lishner, & Catalano, 1985).

In addition to family and peer factors, it is also important to look at broader social factors that may place a youth at risk for problematic usage. For example, a youth's decision to use substances may relate to the school environment. Lack of identification with teachers, an inadequate number of caring and competent teacher models, and dilapidated schools are conducive to higher rates of risk-taking behavior (Felner, 1988; National Institute of Education, 1978). If the only employed, supposedly successful adults in a poor area are pimps and drug abusers, the children and adolescents will have few effective models to emulate, and the chances increase that they will adopt lifestyles similar to that of the drug-abusing adults.

The positive portrayal of drug and alcohol use in the media — in both programming and advertising — may also contribute to adolescent substance use. Alcohol, tobacco, and drug advertisements are pervasive throughout the mass media. The predominant message of advertisements is that use of recreational drugs (e.g., cigarettes, alcohol), or frequent use of over-the-counter drugs (e.g., aspirin, sleeping pills) is not only acceptable but desirable. For example, a current cigarette advertisement depicts a group of young adults happily playing volleyball and smoking cigarettes, with the caption "Be a part of it." This may suggest to youngsters that smoking is a sign of maturity or that it is a necessity for acceptance by one's peers. The mass media plays an important role in adolescents' learning about drugs, and is perceived by them as a trusted source of information (Flay, 1988). This suggests that, particularly if there are gaps in adult role models, at home and/or in the community, adolescents may obtain influential drug-related messages from the media.

In this chapter we have examined some of the factors that may place children and adolescents at risk for later substance abuse. During later childhood and adolescence, parental and societal values are questioned and explored. The struggle for independence and identity occurs within the contexts of families, school systems, and communities. For many youth, these contexts can provide an important network of supports and opportunities for success. It is within these contexts that youth can develop and master the skills to make the successful transition into independent adulthood. For others, however, these arenas may provide limited opportunities for success and poor models of coping. For such youth, risk-taking may become a means of coping, and health-endangering, maladaptive patterns of behavior may develop. In the next chapter, these developmental processes will be examined and incorporated into a model for understanding and predicting substance abuse in children and adolescents. This understanding should, in turn, enable readers to select preventive programs that are sensitive to both the developmental and environmental factors confronting youth.

Chapter 2

Theories of Substance Abuse

So far, we have examined some of the developmental and social forces associated with substance abuse among youth. In this chapter, these principles will be incorporated into a theoretical model from which we can better understand — and predict — substance use and abuse in children and adolescents. We hope that this information will enable readers to more easily interpret and understand published research in the area.

In the following sections, we will review the major psychosocial theories and models of substance abuse. We will then present a social stress model, which integrates current perspectives on substance abuse and provides several new dimensions. We feel that this model will provide readers with a firm foundation for understanding the drug abuse prevention efforts reviewed in chapter 3.

PSYCHOSOCIAL PERSPECTIVES ON DRUG ABUSE

The major psychosocial perspectives that have been advanced to explain substance use include: (a) problem behavior theory (Jessor & Jessor, 1977), (b) social learning theory (Bandura, 1977), (c) stage theory (Kandel, 1980), and (d) the biopsychosocial model (Wills & Shiffman, 1985). Although each perspective emphasizes somewhat different factors and processes, all view substance use as stemming from the interaction of personality, environmental, and behavioral factors. For readers interested in a more extended overview of theories on drug abuse, the National Institute on Drug Abuse has compiled a research monograph that presents a representative selection of contemporary theoretical perspectives in the drug abuse research field (Lettieri, Sayers, & Pearson, 1980).

Most substance abuse prevention strategies (including the skills-based programs in chapter 3) have their theoretical roots in social learning theory and problem behavior theory. From this perspective, substance use behavior is seen as learned through a process of modeling and reinforcement, which is mediated by personal factors such as cognition, attitudes, and beliefs. We will briefly review these theories in order to better understand how they can form the foundations of prevention efforts.

Problem Behavior Theory

Jessor and Jessor (1977, 1980) suggest that the likelihood of drug abuse is predicted by one's overall propensity to problem behavior. Problem behavior refers to behavior that is socially defined as either a problem, a source of concern, or simply undesirable, by the norms or institutions of conventional society (e.g., stealing, aggression, substance use). The occurrence of problem behaviors is determined by the outcome of three interconnected systems — behavior, personality, and perceived social environment. The behavior system is differentiated into a problem behavior structure (including drug use, sexual activity, problem drinking and general deviant behavior) and a conventional behavior structure (including involvement with a church or formalized religious activity and academic achievement). Participation in either system serves as an alternative to engaging in the other. For example, participation in academic activities should relate negatively to substance use or other problem behaviors.

The personality system is composed of three structures, including: (1) the motivational-instigation system (e.g., the expectation for achieving academic goals, independence, and close peer relations), (2) the personal belief structure (e.g., social criticism, alienation, self-esteem, and locus of control), and (3) the personal control system (e.g., tolerance of deviance, religiosity, and the discrepancy between positive and negative functions of problem behaviors).

The perceived environment is separated into proximal and distal structures which are composed of variables that are directly or less directly related to problem behaviors such as drug use. The variables within the distal structures include: (1) perceived support from parents and from peers, (2) perceived controls from parents and from friends, (3) compatibility between parents and peers in their expectations for behavior, and (4) the relative influence of peers versus parents. The proximal structure includes parent and peer approval for problem behavior and peer models for problem behavior.

The Jessor's conceptualization also identifies demographic and socialization factors, but they consider their role minor relative to the personality, perceived environment, and behavioral systems (Jessor, 1979).

Social Learning Theory

Social learning theory (Bandura, 1969, 1977) extends problem behavior theory by suggesting that behavioral patterns will be more or less problematic depending on the opportunities and social influences to which one is exposed, the skillfulness with which one performs, and the balance of rewards one receives from participation in these activities. The rewards one receives for behavior will directly affect the likelihood that one will continue that behavior (Bandura, 1977). These rewards are themselves a function of the opportunities available for participation in groups and activities, as well as the skills an individual applies in his or her behaviors. The risk for problem behavior is thus reduced when youngsters perform skillfully in conventional settings. Substance use is conceptualized as a socially learned, purposeful, and functional behavior which is the result of the interplay of social-environmental and personal factors.

Stage Theory

Substance abuse programs that seek to prevent the usage of particular categories of substances (e.g. tobacco, marijuana, alcohol) are generally based on Kandel's stage theory. Kandel (1980; 1982) suggests a psychosocial perspective in which involvement with drugs proceeds through different stages. Adolescents typically progress sequentially from beer and wine to hard liquor and cigarettes, next to marijuana, and then on to other illicit drugs. Although early involvement does not necessarily lead to the later stages, usage at one stage is very unlikely without usage at the earlier stage.

Kandel's research suggests that somewhat different predictors are important with different types of drugs. Specifically, prior involvement in deviant activities and the use of cigarettes, beer, and wine are most important for predicting hard liquor use. Beliefs and values favorable to the use of marijuana and association with marijuana-using peers are the strongest predictors of initiation into experimentation with marijuana. Poor relations with parents, feelings of depression, heavy marijuana use, unconventional attitudes, and exposure to drug-using peers and role models are most important for predicting initiation into illicit drugs other than marijuana (e.g., cocaine, LSD, amphetamines, heroin).

The Biopsychosocial Model

A new psychosocial perspective on substance abuse is emerging from the field of behavioral medicine and from recent interest in competence and coping (Wills & Shiffman, 1985).

The biopsychosocial model is based on two central premises. The first is that substances may be used as a coping mechanism for two independent reasons: (a) they can reduce negative affect, or (b) they can increase positive affect. Individuals may use a substance to reduce negative affect when they are anxious or over aroused, or they may also use the same substance to enhance positive affect when they are fatigued, depressed, or under aroused. The model suggests that several processes (cognitive, physiological, and stress reaction) may intervene between the occurrence of a potentially stressful event and the occurrence of an adverse reaction (Wills & Shiffman, 1985).

The second premise is that it is useful to distinguish between two types of stress-coping skills: (a) those generic responses that help the individual to deal with a variety of stressors, and (b) those responses that are used to cope with temptations for substance use. Skills to cope with stress (e.g., enduring and daily stressors) are distinguished from skills relevant for coping with temptation (e.g., peer pressure). This model conceptualizes substance abuse as a product of deficiency in coping skills that are relevant to a variety of stressors. When faced with personal or social pressure to use substances, youth with social skills deficits are more likely to engage in usage.

CRITICAL EXAMINATION OF CURRENT THEORETICAL FRAMEWORKS

Overall, current psychosocial theories and models have broadened our understanding of substance abuse and have stimulated extensive research. The theorists tend to place a heavy emphasis on individual personality and coping styles, and the ways that these factors interact to contribute to substance abuse. This emphasis has influenced the focus and scope of current research as well as the prevailing prevention programs. Specifically, current theorists have emphasized a wide range of personal characteristics that may place youth at risk, including: low religiosity, low self-esteem, lack of clear value positions, poor interpersonal relations, poor coping strategies, and difficulties countering pressures to use drugs. Given the focus on the individual, current work in the field of substance abuse prevention tends to highlight the role of person-oriented cognitive and behavioral prevention strategies. At the same time, these models tend to place less emphasis on addressing the ecological factors that may be influencing behavior.

Regrettably, a statement by Blau with reference to social science research made over a quarter of a century ago, is still timely for work with drug abuse. Blau (1960) writes:

> Research has provided much information regarding the influence of attitudes of individuals and their social systems on human behavior, but they have contributed little to our knowledge of the structural constraints exerted by common values and status distributions in groups and communities (p. 178).

In other words, whereas the theories and models provide a comprehensive account of the personal qualities and interrelations of youth and their families, they may be underemphasizing the influence of broader community variables, such as discrimination and the inequitable distribution of resources.

THE SOCIAL STRESS MODEL OF SUBSTANCE ABUSE

In this book, we will be introducing a social stress model, derived from Albee's (1982) model of psychopathology, as an alternative approach to the study of adolescent substance abuse. This model integrates the traditional emphasis on individual and family systemic variables with the recent research on competence and coping. Additionally, in contrast to most theoretical approaches, the social stress model seeks to explicitly address the broader social variables that influence adolescent behavior.

From this perspective, adolescent drug usage is viewed as the long-term outcome of multiple experiences with significant others and social systems from birth through adolescence. A youngster's experiences in the family, school, and community are seen as influencing the identification with parents, peers, and role models and the development of effective coping strategies. Children who (a) have not identified with parent figures and consequently have failed to incorporate their values and standards, (b) have failed to acquire the necessary skills to offset the pressures to use drugs and (c) have not had adequate educational and employment opportunities, may be less certain of their own abilities and less equipped to cope with a variety of social stressors during adolescence. These youth are more likely to be influenced by peers who are in the same situation and may be influenced by such peers to engage in drug use as a means of coping with stress (Elliott, Huizinga, & Ageton, 1982).

Alternately, adolescents will be less likely to engage in problematic early usage as a means of coping with these stressors if (a) they have made positive attachments with their families, teachers, and peers, (b) they have developed adequate coping skills, and (c) have school and community models of competent coping as well as sufficient resources and opportunites. Although we will be using this model to understand the etiology and maintenance of substance abuse among children and adolescents, this general framework can be extended to other problem behaviors, such as delinquency or other excessive risk-taking behaviors. These behaviors can be viewed as ineffective coping strategies.

The risk for substance abuse can be conceptualized as a fractional equation with stress in the numerator and positive attachments, coping skills, and resources in the denominator (see Figure 2.1). This conceptualization is a derivation of Albee's (1982) model of psychopathology, in which the risk for psychopathology is conceived of as a function of stress and organic factors and the extent to which the negative impact of these factors is offset by coping skills, competencies, and social support.

In our application of Albee's model, the likelihood of an adolescent engaging in

$$\frac{\textbf{Stress}}{\textbf{Attachments} + \textbf{Coping Skills} + \textbf{Resources}} = \textbf{Risk for Substance Abuse}$$

FIGURE 2.1. Social coping model of substance abuse.

drug usage is seen as a function of the stress level and the extent to which it is offset by positive attachments, coping skills, and resources. To better understand how this equation can predict a youngster's drug usage, each of these components will be reviewed.

Stress

Researchers have identified several categories or levels of stress and have examined their role in the development of problem behaviors (Tolan, Miller, & Thomas, in press; Tolan & Thomas, 1987; Wills & Shiffman, 1985) including: major life events, daily hassles, enduring life strains, induced transitions, and developmental transitions. The first category consists of major life events such as a car accident or the death of a parent (Dohrenwend & Dohrenwend, 1981). These events frequently occur suddenly and entail an initial period of shock followed by gradual readjustment. For almost all of these events, the child or adolescent has no control over when they occur. Youth may turn to drugs as a means of coping with the pain and disruption caused by any of these events.

A second level of stress consists of everyday problems or "daily hassles," such as arguments over the use of the car or curfew times (DeLongis, Coyne, Dakof, Folkman, & Lazarus, 1982). Swearington and Cohen (1985) suggest that adolescents' problem behaviors are more related to level of day-to-day conflicts and pressures than to more isolated stressful life events. A youngster may use drugs to escape from family or school interactions characterized by chronic conflict.

The third category of stress consists enduring life strains (Pearlin & Schooler, 1978) such as difficulties in the family, the school, and the community. These stressors usually persist over time and are not easily resolved (e.g., a lack of privacy, insufficient opportunities for recreation and employment, or inadequate school conditions). This type of stress is most related to factors in the socioeconomic environment. For example, certain youth may be exposed to poor school or housing situations because of discrimination and the inequitable distribution of societal resources (Albee, 1982). If school is a place where the youngster can obtain few successes and the community provides few models of competent coping, the adolescent may have less confidence in her or his chances for success. To these youth, societal standards of success may appear unreachable, and risk-taking behaviors that flaunt societal expectations become more attractive and appealing.

A fourth category of stressor faced by adolescents includes life transitions that require adaptation over time, such as a transition to a new school, obtaining one's first job, or getting married (Jason & Bogat, 1983). Such transitions may be particulary stressful if they involve interruptions in peer relations. For example, when a family moves to a new community, an adolescent is often faced with the difficult tasks of entering a new school system, interacting with established cliques, and making new friends. Drugs may facilitate acceptance into a new peer group or alleviate heightened levels of social anxiety (Pentz, 1985).

Developmental changes during adolescence (e.g., puberty, adherence to group norms, changing alliances from family to peers) are stressful events, and can be considered the fifth type of stressor. Reductions in self-esteem, pressures to fit in with peers, striving toward independence (including curiosity, need for adventure, and rebellion), can often lead to the initiation of substance use among adolescents.

Taken together, the stressors in an adolescent's life can strongly affect the decision to use drugs or engage in other problem behaviors (Bry, McKeon, & Pandina, 1982; Vaux & Ruggerio, 1983; Tolan, in press). A preventive strategy might involve increasing the adolescent's resistance to the deleterious effects of stress. Such efforts could be focused on promoting positive attachments in the family and school and enhancing social coping skills. In addition, efforts could be taken to limit the level of stress that the young person must experience. Changes in social policy could reduce the impact of enduring strain (Joffe & Albee, 1981); for example, efforts could be made to ensure that adequate education and employment opportunities are available. Similarly, the stress of induced transitions could be reduced through the provision of supportive interventions. For example, those with early signs of academic problems and high levels of life stressors at home, when transferring to a new school could be provided with academic and social assistance to facilitate the transition, and this might help prevent long-term negative academic outcomes and problem behaviors (Jason, Johnson, Betts, Smith, Kruckenberg, & Cradick, 1987).

We will now examine the quotients in the denominator (positive attachments, coping skills, and resources) of Figure 1 that can offset the negative impact of these stressors.

Attachments

Children who have not identified with parental figures, or who have not incorporated their values and standards, may be at greater risk for substance abuse. With gaps in attachment to adult role models and dissatisfaction with support received at home, these youngsters are more likely to associate with youth experiencing similarly difficult home lives. Hawkins and Weiss (1985) explain this process in their social developmental model of behavior. According to this model, attachments or bonds are generally formed within the family, the school, and the peer group. In each of these contexts, three variables influence behavior patterns: (a) the opportunities and influences to which one is exposed, (b) the skillfulness with which one performs, and (c) the relative balance of rewards one receives. These variables determine whether a youth's participation in that context will contribute to the development of a positive attachment with the family, school, and peer group, and increase the likelihood that adolescents will develop a sense of efficacy and control in their interactions.

In the family, where this process begins, youngsters must be provided opportunities for family involvement, develop the required skills to behave as expected, and be rewarded consistently. Positive attachments to school depend on the strength of the attachments to the family, as well as the extent to which the child experiences opportunities for involvements, develops skills, and is rewarded.

Similarly, social attachments to peers, whether prosocial or delinquent, will develop to the extent that youngsters have opportunities for involvement with those peers, the skills to perform as expected, and rewards from their peers (Hawkins et al., 1985). The stronger the attachments to family and school, the less likely it is that youth will develop attachments to drug using peers. The reason for this is clear: the behaviors rewarded in the majority of families and those likely to be rewarded by delinquent youth are not compatible (Elliott et al., 1982; Kandel, 1978).

Skills

Developmental research has indicated that most children and adolescents acquire a broad base of coping and social skills. The emergence of skills accelerates during early adolescence, when school, family, and peer relations are in transition and when there is increased pressure exerted on adolescents by adults to accept responsibility for a variety of interpersonal behaviors and events (Parkes, 1971). The development of skills is to a large extent influenced by the patterns of attachments and stressors that occur during childhood and adolescence. That is, children who have been provided with opportunities to learn appropriate skills, have been consistently rewarded for effective coping, and have not been exposed to debilitating stressors are more likely to acquire a comprehensive set of adaptive skills.

Wills and Shiffman (1985) have distinguished several different *cognitive* and *behavioral* coping strategies that might apply to various types of problems faced by adolescents. Coping responses represent potential resources, any of which may be called on to deal with a particular problem. For example, young people whose parents are undergoing a divorce may feel confused and stressed, and may be at greater risk for substances abuse. To the extent that they can access and use effective coping skills, they will be less likely to use drugs as a means of coping with the social anxiety. *Cognitive* strategies that could be used to cope with such stress include: (a) self-assurance — assuring oneself that one can handle the problem; (b) downward comparison — assuring oneself that one is in some way better off than others; (c) restructuring — reinterpreting the problem in a more positive light; and (d) self control — remembering previous successes, thinking about the negative consequences of performing an undesired behavior, or exerting willpower not to do something.

According to Wills and Shiffman (1985), *behavioral* coping strategies involve active attempts to make a decision and change the problem situation. Behavioral strategies that can be used to cope with a stressor include: (a) problem solving — gathering information relevant to the problem, evaluating alternative courses of action, and making a decision to pursue a particular course; (b) direct action — attempting to change the situation through action, negotiation, or compromises; (c) withdrawal — physically leaving the situation or avoiding such situations altogether; (d) assertiveness — using appropriate assertive behavior in social situations; (e) seeking social support — actively seeking help from others to cope with the problem; (f) alternatives — intentionally engaging in alternative behaviors incompatible with the problematic behavior; and finally (g) relaxation — reducing one's response to stress through relaxation exercises, or meditation.

The above skills represent a broad range of cognitive and behavioral competencies, any or all of which could be used by a youth to cope with stress. Therefore, the social stress model and the biopsychosocial model (Wills & Shiffman, 1985) posit that possession, by children and adolescents, of a broad repertoire of coping strategies and the ability to use them to cope with stress will lower the likelihood of substance abuse.

Resources

Youthful risk-taking behaviors are also influenced by a wide array of resources in the community. The school and neighborhood are constant sources of information, which influences behavior both directly and indirectly. If the school and the community provide adequate models of success and coping and society's standards of success appear obtainable, then the adolescent may have more hopes for success. In such cases, the available opportunities for education, employment, and rewarding activity may provide the necessary alternatives that reduce the risk for abusing substances.

On the other hand, youth confronted with inadequate and deficient resources may be at greater risk for substance abuse. To be more concrete, dropout rates in many inner-city schools are staggering and the unemployment rates in poverty areas are excessive, particularly among minorities. Those youth living in such poverty-infested areas often do not earn basic educational credentials, and thus have few employment opportunities. Without such resources and positive role models in the community, these youth may be more at risk for using drugs (Felner, 1988).

The Transaction of the Variables

We have reviewed several ways of controlling stress, involving attachments, coping skills, and resources, and we have suggested how they relate to the risk for substance abuse. It is important to note that these variables often transact with each other to offset the impact of stress. For example, consistent and caring parents and teachers may lead to acquisition of effective coping skills, and facilitate the development of hardy, resilient youth. Hardy youth interpret threats as challenges, view their environment and stressors as within their control or influence, and have a sense of personal commitment (Kobasa, 1979). Such adolescents perceive difficulties as less threatening, and cope with stress more effectively, than do other, less competent youth (Hobfoll, in press). Similarly, healthy developmental functioning and positive relations with parents have been shown to contribute to resilience among high-risk youth (Werner & Smith, 1982). Finally, the ways in which one interprets and copes with stress may influence the ability to access resources in the community and select appropriate models of success (see Figure 2.2).

An understanding of the various components of the equation and the ways in

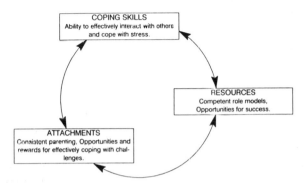

FIGURE 2.2. Transaction of variables.

which they transact should enable us to make predictions about which adolescents may abuse substances. Specifically, depending on the relative balance of the equation, young people may either turn to early drug use as a means of coping with stress or utilize more effective social coping strategies to avoid the temptation, peer pressure, and high risk behavior settings conducive to the abuse of drugs.

Some children may engage in drug use to reduce stress arising from poor relations with parents and teachers, deficient coping skills, or inadequate resources in the school and community. The use of drugs under such circumstances may alleviate stress for a short time. This model is supported by studies showing decreases in anxiety or depression following drug use, at least for drug use assessed over short-term periods of 6 months or less (Aneshensel & Huba, 1983). If initial experimentation leads to more regular usage, however, there are increases rather than decreases in stress over the long-term. If the youngsters use drugs as a coping mechanism, they are inhibited from learning more adaptive social coping skills (Pentz, 1985). In addition, chronic use is likely to preclude close attachments to parents, teachers, and prosocial peers as well as access to positive resources in the community. Thus, social coping skills and adaptive behaviors are expected to decrease as a consequence of heavy drug use (Wrubel, Brenner, & Lazarus, 1981).

Alternately, youth who are experiencing lower levels of stress, or who have sufficient attachments, skills, and resources to effectively offset the impact of stress may be less likely to begin substance use in childhood and early adolescence. These youth may use substances later in adolescence as a function of social pressures and experimentation with lifestyles. This later initiation is typically associated with more limited patterns of usage and a reduced risk for later serious abuse (Robins & Przybeck, 1985) (see Figure 2.3); of course, later initiation does not always preclude more serious abuse, nor does early initiation necessarily lead to abuse. These two pathways, however, are far less likely and predictive of the final outcome than the general pathways described above (Robins & Przybeck, 1985).

These two more likely pathways described above suggest that substances may

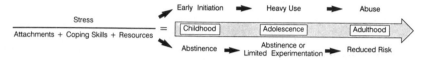

FIGURE 2.3. Social coping model of substance abuse: The outcomes.

serve different functions for different adolescents. For those who are under severe stress or can not effectively cope with stress, early substance use often functions as a coping mechanism. Our model suggests, however, that if the youngster continues to use substances as a coping mechanism rather than progressing to more limited use, a cycle of abuse may emerge that further alienates the youth from the very contexts that may provide resources and competent models of coping. For adolescents who can generally cope well with stress or have sufficient resources to offset the impact of stress, substances may be used later in adolescence as a way to handle normative social and developmental pressures.

The social stress model suggests that in addition to focusing on individual, family, and peer variables, we need to examine the large-scale social, political, and economic issues that may impact on substance use. For example, the school and community are constant sources of information that affect youthful behavior. Thus, in addition to attempting to influence the adolescent, our efforts should also be focused on influencing school and social policies. Such issues often seem overwhelming and futile. Indeed, some of the leaders in the field of prevention have argued that mental health professionals should avoid "vague, ponderous, infeasible giant steps" and concentrate instead on "concrete, achievable, baby steps" (Cowen, 1977).

The social stress model of substance abuse suggests that both baby steps and giant steps are important. Concrete steps that seek to enhance youths' ability to interact within their social contexts and successfully cope with the stressors of adolescence can reduce the risk for problem behavior. Programs that seek to enhance youths' ability to cope with stress and resist peer pressure, for example, have been positively evaluated for their ability to decrease substance usage among youth (see Botvin, 1985a, 1985b). At the same time, our model suggests that we should more closely examine the broader social context and attempt to influence it in such a way as to minimize the social and institutional obstacles to youthful adjustment. For example, efforts could be taken to improve the quality of school systems.

Broader variables, such as socioeconomic status (SES), race, school environments, and community resources have rarely been considered of central interest by researchers involved in the field of drug abuse. These variables, however, can provide important information concerning the adolescents' risk for substance abuse. For example, in an extensive review, Rutter and Gilder (1984) found SES to be a significant factor in problem behavior among youth. They suggested that lower SES can increase the impact of other stressors (Rutter & Gilder, 1984). Levels of substance usage have also been related to race. Higher rates of drug abuse and use have been found among Hispanic and Black adolescents (Padilla, Padilla, Morales, Olnedo, & Ramirez, 1979), and the rate of substance usage among American Indians is between two and three times higher than that of other adolescents (Bobo, 1986).

There is also evidence that a school's climate can influence both academic achievement and student behavior (Felner, Ginter, & Primavera, 1982). The Safe School Study (National Institute of Education, 1978) concluded that some schools have adopted policies which have lowered rates of problem behavior. These schools that have been successful have had the following characteristics: their courses are relevant and interesting, students are recognized for their achievements, student–teacher contact is at high levels, and students have more control over what happens to them. What these findings suggest is that in addition to looking at individual, family, and peer variables, we should also consider the influences and limitations imposed by societal factors (Simcha-Fagen & Schwartz, 1986).

The social stress model is consistent with the existing empirical evidence, reviewed in the previous chapter, on the etiology of adolescent drug use and abuse. The model provides a framework for proposing and assessing interventions that seek to delay the onset of drug use, to prevent regular use, and to prevent drug abuse among adolescents. The model suggests comprehensive strategies for all levels of the problem. Efforts can be taken to reduce the level of stress; at the same time, interventions designed to facilitate positive attachments to the family and school system and enhance social coping skills can offset its harmful effects. Finally, efforts can be taken to influence social policy and institutions that impact on youthful substance abuse. In the following chapter, we will present examples of each of these prevention strategies, ranging from drug education and skill-building programs to more community-based interventions.

Chapter 3

Preventive Interventions for Children and Adolescents

Collectively, our nation's substance abuse prevention efforts are often referred to as a "war on drugs." Given this terminology, it is possible to imagine the world of substance abuse as a battlefield. As far as one can see, from horizon to horizon, there are casualties. There are the victims of traffic accidents, suicides, and a range of academic and social problems. To counter the devastating impact of drugs, a wide variety of preventive strategies are brought to the battle. Armed with an understanding of the risk factors, these strategies have become increasingly sophisticated and effective. At the same time, many of the factors that we discussed in the previous chapters have rarely been addressed by prevention programs. A developmental perspective, such as the one presented in chapter 1, and an overall etiological model, such as the social stress model presented in chapter 2, are critical for our understanding of the current drug abuse problem among youth. To intervene without a careful consideration of the many issues previously discussed might be ill advised.

In general, there have been three existing primary prevention strategies for children and adolescents: drug information/education, skills training, and community-based prevention programs. The theoretical base and effectiveness of programs using these approaches will be reviewed in this chapter. In our analysis of these programs, we will interpret the findings from a theoretical position that integrates many of the developmental, stress, and ecological concepts that have been previously introduced.

INFORMATION AND EDUCATION PROGRAMS

Traditional drug education programs provide students with information regarding the health hazards and social consequences of taking drugs. The rationale behind this approach is that adolescents simply need to be provided with the necessary factual information. Once aware of the relevant facts, they can, and presumably will, choose to adopt healthy lifestyle patterns. Although these programs have led to increases in knowledge, they have been ineffective in decreasing substance usage (Schaps, Bartolo, Moskowitz, Palley, & Churgin, 1981; Berberin, Gross, Lovejoy, & Paparella, 1976) and have in fact been associated with an increase in experimentation (Gordon & McAlister, 1982). There are several reasons for this limited success.

First, most of the programs are based on the assumption that youth begin to smoke, drink, or use drugs because they are unaware of the potential risks. Research has indicated, however, that substance behavior is related to a variety of factors, not simply the absence of knowledge about the health, social, and legal risks. As Gordon and McAlister (1982) observed:

> Probably the most important reason that this type of approach does not have a stronger impact on adolescent drinking is that it does not leave room for discussion of the variety of reasons for which people use alcohol and other mood-altering substances — as a rite of passage; to prove sexuality; to relieve boredom; to escape from pressure; to facilitate social interactions; to solve personal problems; to relieve anxiety, depression or fatigue; to satisfy curiosity or needs for adventure, conformity, rebellion or self-exploration; or for pleasure. The emotional and physiological changes of puberty make adolescents extremely susceptible to psychosocial pressures to engage in many high-risk activities in order to achieve status in their peer group, even if the activities have known undesirable health consequences (p. 212).

Second, developmental research has shown that whereas children and young adolescents are likely to adopt the opinions of respected adults; adolescents, who are entering a higher level of cognitive processing and developing a strong identification with adult behavior, are more likely to respond to inconsistencies in adult cigarette and alcohol attitudes and behaviors, especially attitudes and behaviors regarding teenage smoking and drinking (Gordon & McAlister, 1982). In other words, children and adolescents may question adults' messages against smoking when they observe that their parents smoke cigarettes.

A third problem with an informational approach is that there are contradictory findings concerning some of the immediate and long-term physical, mental, and social effects of some substances. For example, recent research suggests that moderate alcohol use may actually protect against certain chronic diseases (LaPorte, Cresanta, & Kuller, 1980). A teenager hearing these reports in the media may generalize this to all substances and then feel invulnerable to the development of future personal and health problems as a result of occasional usage (Gordon & McAlister, 1982).

Additionally, some adolescents may find that the information presented in the educational programs contradicts their own experiences. For example, a recent television advertisement depicts eggs frying in a pan and draws an analogy to the effects of drugs on the brain. This may run contrary to the experience of many adolescents, and ultimately this unrealistic message may reduce the believability of entire drug related campaigns.

PSA—C

Despite the questionable etiological basis for this approach, as well as over a decade of research indicating that information alone does not deter or decrease substance use, drug education continues to be the most widely used approach to preventing adolescent substance abuse (Botvin, 1985a). The question naturally arises as to why traditional drug education programs continue to be implemented in many school systems. It is likely that many public officials are not familiar with this research literature and more effective approaches. Government officials, agencies, and school administrators are thus probably satisfied with this approach, which is generally inexpensive and easily delivered.

The relative failure of informational approaches to prevent substance use and abuse has led to a broadening of the scope of substance abuse prevention programs and the development of more comprehensive, skills-based strategies.

SKILLS-BASED STRATEGIES

Skills-based strategies seek to enhance the social coping skills of youth in order to offset the influences and pressures to use drugs. The first skills-based programs focused specifically on cigarettes and the social pressures to smoke (Evans, Hansen, & Mittlemark, 1977; Jason, 1977). The programs incorporated strategies to "socially inoculate" the students and increase assertive behavior to prevent the onset of smoking. The social inoculation strategy was borrowed from the medical disease prevention model, in which the individual is exposed to small, repeated doses of the disease to provide an immunity against subsequent development. Psychological inoculation exposes the youth to some of the situations where pressure to smoke may be salient.

Programs developed by Evans and his colleagues at Baylor College of Medicine have repeatedly used psychological inoculation, with varying degrees of success. Evans et al. (1977) postulated that there are three main sources of pressure to smoke in children's environments. Most influential were peer pressure, parental pressure, and coercive media messages. By gradually exposing children to social settings where pressure to smoke may exist, they have time to formulate and practice strategies to use in the future when faced with peer pressure to engage in smoking. In these programs, the emphasis is not on convincing the adolescent not to smoke. Rather, through repeated exercises, such as role playing and practice, the youth develop skills to resist external pressure to smoke.

Skills-based smoking prevention programs have also focused on role playing, assertiveness training, and cognitive modeling to prevent smoking among youngsters. From 1976 to 1980, investigators at DePaul University used a variety of these types of behavioral strategies with inner-city children in Chicago to prevent the onset of smoking and reduce current levels of smoking (Jason, 1977; Jason, 1979; Jason, Mollica, & Ferone, 1982; Spitzzeri & Jason, 1979). For example, Jason et. al. (1982) implemented a six-week role-playing and assertiveness training program for all ninth graders within an inner-city high school. At a 17-month follow-up, over 50 percent of the previous smokers who had been provided the skills-based program were abstinent, whereas none of the smokers in the control school were abstinent.

Other programs have made peers the primary change agents. For example, the CLASP (Counseling Leadership Against Smoking Pressure) project used peers as leaders in a program that promoted the development of group strategies for coping with peer pressure (McAlister, Perry, & Macoby, 1980). After 2 years, the youth exposed to this program began smoking at less than half the rate of those who received no program.

Overall, psychological inoculation, role playing, cognitive modeling, and peer led assertion training have all been utilized, with varying degrees of success, to offset interpersonal pressure to smoke. It has been suggested, however, that young people with fewer environmental resources and life skills may be less successful in resisting the interpersonal pressures to smoke (Schinke & Gilchrist, 1984). Subsequent smoking prevention programs have addressed this important issue by including an even wider range of coping skills such as self-control and problem-solving skills (Schinke & Gilchrist, 1983; Botvin & Wills, 1985).

More recently, skills training approaches have been incorporated into programs that focus on a variety of drugs. For example, since 1980, researchers at DePaul University have been implementing a skills-based substance abuse prevention program in inner-city Chicago elementary schools. The program, which is targeted at seventh and eighth graders, provides students with instruction and modeling as well as extensive opportunities for role playing. The program seeks to enhance the students' general coping skills as well as those more specifically focused on drug-related issues. Evaluations have indicated decreases in substance use, as well as improvements in a variety of cognitive and behavioral skills (Beaulieu, & Jason, in press; Dupont & Jason, 1984; Rhodes & Jason, 1987).

Some of the most well-known programs in the area of skills-based substance abuse prevention have been conducted by Pentz (at the University of Tennessee and University of Southern California), Flay (at the University of Waterloo and the University of Southern California), Johnson and Hansen (at the University of Southern California), Gilchrist and Schinke (at the University of Washington), and Botvin (at Cornell University). In the following sections we will review the rationale, techniques, and evaluation of these programs. These approaches each presume slightly different causes of drug abuse, although all are consistent in viewing the problems as a deficit in the potential users (see also the reviews of Flay, 1985; Botvin & Wills, 1985; Botvin, 1986).

A focus on skills deficits has led to the development of standardized skills-based programs that can be implemented and evaluated in classroom settings. Although this focus on individual skills training has facilitated dissemination and evaluation, this approach does have limitations. Not all children who are unskilled or socially incompetent become substance users. Similarly, some socially skilled children begin to experiment with substances. In these cases, it may not be a skills deficit that accounts for the behavior, but other ecological factors in the adolescent's home, school, or community setting. It is these forces that may need to be addressed by the substance abuse prevention program. These types of programs will be reviewed in a later section. Nonetheless, the reader should be familiar with the skills-based programs, as this approach represents a vast improvement over the more limited education-only model reviewed previously.

Social Assertiveness Skills Training (Pentz et al.)

Pentz, Cormack, Flay, Hansen, and Johnson (1986) have developed a Student Taught Awareness and Resistance (STAR) skills approach that is based on a social competence model of substance abuse. According to this model, substance use in early adolescence is the result of social influences, such as peer and parent usage, and poor social assertiveness skills with which to resist pressures to use substances. This model is based on etiological findings that have found correlations between adolescent substance use and (a) parent and peer substance use; (b) cognitive variables, such as low self-efficacy; (c) problem behaviors, such as school failure, delinquency, and aggression, (d) stress, and (e) low social support from adults.

These findings suggest that students with lower social competence may be more likely to use substances as a means of coping with social anxiety. In addition, these students may be less able to resist and counter social pressures to use substances. Based on these assumptions, Pentz (1985) has developed a preventive intervention that seeks to increase students' social competence and self-efficacy. The program is based on cognitive-behavior therapy and, more specifically, assertiveness skill training. The program consists of ten 55-minute sessions, which are conducted by a trained teacher paired with a program assistant and facilitated by peer leaders, who are identified by their classmates and provided leadership training. Skills relevant to several social situations are demonstrated and taught through modeling, rehearsal, and feedback. Students first learn key concepts and practice identifying pressure situations. Students then observe role models demonstrating simple techniques for resisting pressure. Finally, students practice the resistance skills and apply them to a variety of situations. The curriculum contains 10 lessons including: (a) introduction; (b) understanding the consequences of drug use and non-use; (c) learning the facts about drugs; (d) knowing how to say "no"; (e) resisting peer pressure; (f) changing norms to non-use; (g) identifying advertising influences; (h) developing anti-drug commercials; (i) identifying adult influences; and (j) videotaping students resisting drug offers. The program includes a student manual and workbook, a parent workbook, student/parent workbooks, community outreach projects, and technical assistance.

Evaluation of this type of intervention have indicated that children provided with these strategies have shown increased social competence and better grades (Pentz, 1985), and decreased drug use (Pentz, 1985; Pentz et al., 1986; Pentz, Dwyer, Flay, Hansen, Johnson, Mackinnon, & Wang, 1988; Hansen, Johnson, Flay, Graham, & Sobel, in press). These findings indicate that the intervention program is most effective when conducted just before periods of induced transitions (e.g., beginning of junior high school, beginning of high school). The results reported by Pentz support her hypothesized model of substance use and are consistent with the theoretical rationale for the intervention program.

Cognitive–Behavioral Skills Training (Schinke & Gilchrist)

Schinke and Gilchrist (1984) have proposed a cognitive–behavioral substance abuse prevention program. The program is derived from their extensive research in the area of pregnancy prevention (Gilchrist & Schinke, 1985a; Schinke & Gilchrist, 1977). The researchers consider a variety of problem behaviors (drug abuse, unwanted pregnancies, and so forth) from a developmental and social learning theory perspective.

They believe that adolescents should be systematically taught the skills necessary to enjoy positive lives and avoid unnecessary risks (Schinke & Gilchrist, 1984). The cognitive–behavioral approach is thus designed to enable adolescents to acquire the social coping skills necessary for them to "handle current problems, anticipate and prevent future ones, and advance their mental health, social function, economic welfare, and physical well-being" (Schinke & Gilchrist, 1984, p. 33). Schinke and Gilchrist have developed strategies aimed at enhancing such skills as decisionmaking, problem solving, and interpersonal communications in a variety of social situations.

Their eight session, one-hour intervention strategy generally includes (a) providing accurate, relevant information; (b) teaching students a problem-solving strategy to handle a broad range of problem situations; (c) teaching techniques to promote self control; (d) teaching relaxation and coping strategies for relieving stress, anxiety, and pressure; and (e) developing assertiveness skills. Modeling, feedback, reinforcement, coaching, and assignments are utilized to teach and promote practice of these skills (Gilchrist & Schinke, 1985b).

The programs developed by Gilchrist and Schinke have consistently demonstrated the effectiveness of the cognitive–behavioral approach to substance abuse prevention. In addition, this approach has produced significant improvements in several measures of problem solving, decision making, and assertiveness skills as well as knowledge, attitudes, and intentions (Schinke & Blythe, 1981; Schinke & Gilchrist, 1983; Schinke & Gilchrist, 1985).

Life Skills Training (Botvin)

Botvin (1985a) and his colleagues have developed a curriculum-based program called Life Skills Training (LST), which seeks to facilitate the development of generic life skills as well as skills and knowledge more specifically related to substance use. The LST program incorporates a curriculum to teach a wide range of personal and social skills in order to improve youth's general competence and reduce potential motivations for substance use. Specific applications of these skills are practiced in social pressure situations.

The general cognitive–behavioral skills incorporated into the LST Program include techniques for (a) enhancing self-esteem (e.g., goal setting, behavioral change techniques, increasing positive self-statements); (b) resisting persuasive appeals (e.g., identifying persuasive appeals, formulating counter-arguments); (c) coping with anxiety (e.g., relaxation training, mental rehearsal); (d) verbal and non-verbal communication skills; and (e) a variety of other social skills (e.g. initiating social interactions, communication skills, complimenting, assertiveness skills). These skills are taught using a combination of instruction, modeling, and rehearsal. The LST program also teaches students skills and knowledge more specifically related to the problem of substance abuse. For example, in addition to teaching students general assertiveness skills, students are taught how to use these skills to resist direct interpersonal pressure to use drugs.

Evaluations indicate that the LST program is capable of producing initial reductions of 50% or more in new cigarette smoking among junior high school students. In the most recent study conducted, the LST prevention program has also been found to have a significant impact on both drinking and marijuana use (Botvin, 1985b). Moreover, this prevention approach has produced significant changes in knowledge and attitudes relating to smoking, alcohol, and marijuana use. Students' assertiveness, social anxiety, self-esteem, and decisionmaking have also changed as a function of participating in the program. These changes have been in a direction consistent with the theory underlying this prevention model, which posits that the development of generic social coping skills, as well as the transfer of information and skills related more directly to social influences to smoke, drink or use drugs, can decrease substance abuse among adolescents.

General Discussion

These models reviewed above represent a broader-based approach to substance abuse prevention than the earlier social inoculation approaches. These prevention models are all derived from similar theoretical roots, and utilize similar intervention techniques. Substance abuse prevention is approached directly and indirectly through interventions designed to improve social coping skills, and the specific application of these skills to resisting pressures to use substances (Botvin & Wills, 1985). These approaches have produced significant reductions in the use of one or more substances. In addition, these studies have assessed the impact of the prevention programs on mediating variables, and they have been able to demonstrate effects on a number of these variables. The programs developed and evaluated by these research groups provide evidence for the effectiveness of the social skills training substance abuse prevention models (Botvin & Wills, 1985).

Practical Limitations. There are a number of practical problems that may limit the ability of this approach to produce enduring changes in patterns of substance use. The difficulties can be classified as problems relating to (a) complexity, (b) cost, (c) dissemination, (d) target population, and (e) focus of the programs.

COMPLEXITY. In programs that seek to address a wide range of skills, the practitioner may find that there is not enough time to do a thorough job in each area. Consequently, each skill might only be given a superficial introduction. Findings from the smoking cessation literature suggest that studies with simpler treatment programs have resulted in better outcomes than more complex programs (Lando, 1981; Danaher, 1977). Adolescents receiving a complex intervention such as some of the ones described above may feel overwhelmed by the number of behavior changes being introduced.

COST. Another limitation concerns cost. Most of the programs reviewed above, and many of the programs that are currently being implemented across the country, require that the school or agency purchase a "package." This package generally includes teacher manuals and student guides, as well as audiovisual supplements and expert consulting fees. Depending on the number of participants included in the intervention and the setting's prevention budget, the cost of conducting one of these packaged programs may be prohibitive. Thus, it is doubtful that many of the more sophisticated skills-based programs will ever reach the vast majority of the nation's students. Regardless of whether purchased as a package or developed within the setting, most of the skills-based programs also tend to be costly in terms of time. The programs are frequently implemented by outside consultants, and intervention contact time reported in studies has varied from 7 to 20 hours (Glasgow & McCaul, 1985).

DISSEMINATION. It may be more difficult, even with a detailed and well-developed training manual, to train group leaders in this approach than it is for the simpler inoculation prevention programs. Although practitioners may have broad outlines, they do not always have the training or hands-on experience to deal with the day-to-day problems that may arise. For example, researchers have speculated that poor implementation may be responsible for the lack of effect of their teacher-led skills-based interventions (Glasgow & McCaul, 1985).

TARGET POPULATION. Virtually all of the skills-based substance abuse prevention curricula are targeted to white, middle-class populations, and thus most of the research has been conducted with this population. A large proportion of the nation's substance users, however, are lower SES and minority students. Some social skills, for example, most notably decision making and effective communication, are inseparable from personal and cultural values. For example, the need to establish and maintain eye contact is commonly emphasized during communication skills training. Yet within some cultures, children are taught that in certain situations such behavior is discourteous (Bobo, 1986). Thus, current skills-based programs may be unable to provide culturally sensitive, credible curricula for all youth.

FOCUS. Overall, the practical limitations discussed above relate to the broader issue discussed earlier — the tendency of this approach to focus almost exclusively on the adolescents and their coping skills. As the social stress model suggests (see chapter 2), coping skills constitute only one component of the overall drug abuse equation. Specifically, while a repertoire of coping skills is critical in offsetting the negative impact of stress, poor relations with parents and teachers, a lack of resources in the community, and excessive levels of stress can also have a profound impact on a youth's decision to use substances. For example, some students participating in the program may live with alcoholic parents. These youngsters may enjoy learning and practicing the skills for one hour per week, and may actually demonstrate short-term improvements. Nonetheless, the critical components of the program are competing with pervasive influences in the environment. Such youth may have few opportunities beyond the training session to practice and be rewarded for the skills learned; in fact, they may actually be rewarded for behaviors that are incompatible with those promoted in the classroom. Under such circumstances, the maintenance and generalizability of the program effects may be limited.

In addition to these practical limitations, there are several methodological problems which may compromise the internal validity of the studies reviewed above as well as other skills-based programs.

Methodological Shortcomings. Most published program evaluations, as well as all of the studies reviewed above, draw conclusions about the ability of the programs to reduce substance usage. There are, however, several methodological problems associated with measuring substance usage (see chapter 5 for a more extended discussion of this issue). Self-reports of substance usage are frequently biased by inconsistent and inhibited reporting (Rhodes & Jason, 1987). Some of the programs reviewed above attempted to control for these biases through the collection of biological samples, whereas others have relied exclusively on self-reports. This variation in assessment procedures compromises our ability to make meaningful comparisons across studies.

Another important methodological issue concerns both the method of assignment and the unit of analysis. In most of the studies reviewed above, there was random assignment to the treatment or control conditions. The unit of assignment, however, has varied from schools to classes to individuals. Many of the studies that have used the school or classroom as the unit of assignment have conducted statistical analysis at the individual level, thus confounding potential school or classroom differences with treatment effects (Botvin & Wills, 1985).

Another problem that may compromise internal validity and our ability to interpret the results of these and other studies is the problem occurring when students drop out of the program. Most studies do not report whether or not there was differential dropping out among students (i.e., more drug users dropping out as compared to nonusers), rendering it impossible to discern if differential attrition compromised the internal validity of these studies (Botvin & Wills, 1985).

Finally, all of the programs reviewed above and the majority of published evaluation studies were overseen by highly motivated researchers. It will be important to determine the extent to which skills-based prevention programs can be effective without the involvement of the researcher (i.e., when implemented entirely by school personnel or other individuals in the community).

Although there are practical, methodological, and budgetary shortcomings associated with the skills-based approaches, this model will be the most appropriate for many settings. As noted earlier, it is a significant improvement over the earlier drug education approach. To the extent that the programs focuses largely on the adolescent; however, the skills-based approach may be limited in its ability to produce enduring changes in patterns of substance use among youth.

COMMUNITY-BASED PREVENTION

Community-based programs attempt to influence not only the adolescent but also the ecological variables that influence substance usage. By integrating preventive efforts in the family, the school, the community, and the media, this approach addresses the individual as well as the broader social and environmental quotients of the drug abuse equation.

The concept of moving beyond the classroom and the individual is appealing, given the enormous influence of the family, community, and mass media. Adolescents spend a majority of their time outside of school, and most drug use occurs outside of school. Those young people at highest risk of using drugs are least likely to be at school on the days that prevention curricula are delivered (Johnson & Solis, 1983). Absenteeism and dropout rates are highest among adolescent drug users (Friedman, 1985b). Youngsters spend most of their time in the home (as much as 17 hours per day, more on weekends), and these are settings where poor family management and communication factors can lead to drug abuse. In addition, many young people spend a large portion of their time at home watching television (averaging about four to six hours per day), where sexuality, drug-taking, and other risk-taking activities are positively portrayed.

For these reasons, we might need to consider programs that move beyond the individual and the classroom to more directly involve the family, media, and community. These programs may hold the greatest promise for affecting the decision to experiment with and abuse drugs.

Family Involvement in Substance Abuse Prevention

Given the influence that families have on child and adolescent behavior, it is noteworthy how seldom they have been included in substance abuse prevention programs. Bry (1983) reviewed research on this topic, and she concluded that family involvement is very important, if not essential, for positive outcomes in substance abuse prevention programs. Bry found that when families are included in school or media-based interventions, risk-factors can be reduced, family-management practices can be modified, and early signs of problems can be reversed. For example, DeMarsh and Kumpfer (1985) developed an effective prevention program for children and adolescents that focused on including the parent and family in the positive socialization of the child, while also strengthening the family. Several other health promotion programs have highlighted the family or the parents as the main target for the intervention (Downey, Butcher, Frank, Webber, Miner, & Berenson, in press; Nader, Sallis, Rupp, Atkins, Patterson, & Abramson, 1986). These programs have supplemented a clinic- or a school-based program by sending material, directly educating, and screening for risk factors (Murray, Perry, & Davis-Hearn, in press).

Media Involvement in Substance Abuse Prevention

Flay (1988) has studied the role of the mass media in preventing substance abuse among adolescents. His findings suggest that media campaigns must not only give information but also provide skills to help teenagers resist other media influences (e.g., pro-drug messages, TV advertising) (Flay & Sobel, 1983). A comprehensive prevention campaign might combine mass media programming, involvement of families, training of teachers, and advocacy efforts by children. For example, children in schools throughout an entire community could draw posters concerning anti-drug topics or write letters to media personalities asking them not to smoke on television. The children could share their experiences with their families and ask those parents who smoke to participate in an ongoing community smoking-cessation effort described below. A television station could arrange to reward these activities (e.g., an award for the best essay or drawing). Community groups could also participate by advocacy campaigns (e.g., assessing the number of stores that sell cigarettes to minors and then publicizing the findings). Such a broad-based media prevention effort, in combination with a school-based skills program, might represent a more potent approach, by activating an entire community in support of the types of comprehensive changes needed to deal with the drug abuse problems affecting our communities.

Jason, Gruder, Martino, Flay, Warnecke, and Thomas (1987) provide evidence for the effectiveness of a comprehensive media campaign, although more limited than the example above. The researchers worked with several Chicago agencies to implement a "Freedom From Smoking in 20 Days" program that was broadcast on the city's evening news. Approximately one-half million viewers watched this 3-week program. Over 50,000 self-help manuals were distributed to the public. In addition to the media campaign, twice weekly meetings were established at worksettings for employees. Overall, 41% of the participants who used the manuals, watched the series of televised smoking cessation programs, and attended support groups at worksettings stopped smoking at program end. For those provideed with only the media program and the self-help manuals, only 21% quit by program end. Taking 20% as a conservative estimate of the percent of smokers who quit, this program helped 10,000 individuals in Chicago to quit smoking.

We have reviewed several programs that focus not only on the young, but also their families and the communities where they live. Ideally, community-based approaches should be comprehensive and integrated, combining skills training for the adolescent with efforts to positively influence the family, school, and community.

Comprehensive community-based strategies have been well developed for heart disease prevention (the Stanford Five City Project, Maccoby & Alexander, 1979; the North Karelia Project, Puska, McAlister, Pekkola, & Koskela, 1981). The strategies developed and implemented in these programs are applicable to substance abuse prevention programs (Johnson & Solis, 1983). Several promising, comprehensive, community-based programs for drug abuse prevention are underway, including those in Chicago (Rhodes & Jason, 1987); Charlotte, N.C. (Kim, 1982); and Ventura, California (National Institute on Drug Abuse, 1982); and Minnesota (Perry, Klepp, & Shultz, in press).

In the next section, we will review the program of this type that we are most familiar with; the Operation Snowball Substance Abuse Prevention Program.

Operation Snowball

Operation Snowball is a substance abuse prevention program that was designed by students, teachers, parents, and community members in Illinois in 1977. Currently, there are over 70 local Operation Snowball chapters within Illinois. These chapters sponsor three-day retreats, in which high school students receive training in a variety of problem-solving and helping skills and a variety of followup activities throughout the school year.

Operation Snowball Retreat. The Operation Snowball retreats occur at rural centers throughout the state. The retreats are organized and implemented by a community task force, parents, teachers, and students. The students receive scholarships from corporations within the community to help pay for their retreat registration fee. Each chapter's retreat includes general and small group sessions, mini-workshops, and a variety of recreation activities. Typically, the retreats include six general sessions: (a) an introduction; (b) the social and health consequences of substance abuse; (c) social and communication skills (e.g., initiating social interactions, conversation skills, listening); (d) family issues (e.g., techniques for more effective coping with family difficulties); (e) decision making (e.g., techniques for making decisions and achieving goals); and (f) an open invitation to parents (parents are invited to the final general session for an open discussion of issues and concerns).

Participants are also assigned to a small group, which provides a setting for discussions and the exchange of problem-solving and support among the participants. A series of workshops are also organized and implemented throughout the retreat, consisting of (a) a substance abuse workshop, where techniques for coping with and preventing substance use and abuse are practiced; (b) a minority issues workshop, where participants are sensitized to some of the concerns facing minority youth; (c) a peer pressure workshop, offering techniques for resisting peer pressure to use drugs; (d) an anxiety workshop, where strategies for coping with anxiety are reviewed; (e) a stress workshop, including approaches to stressors such as death, divorce, and transitions; and (f) a health promotion workshop, where participants review efforts to improve their fitness and nutrition. The workshops all involve the teaching of personal and social skills, and provide problem-solving support in order to improve participants' general competence and reduce potential motivations for substance use.

Overall, the weekend is viewed as a lever for extensive substance abuse prevention activities in both the junior high and high school, the family, and the community (Resnick & Gibbs, 1983). On returning to their respective schools, the program participants, along with parents, teachers, and community members, are encouraged to engage in followup activities. The activities may include an ongoing skills training seminar for all students, in which skills are practiced and reinforced. In addition, a range of activities are planned, some of which are discussed below.

YOUTH SKILLS PROGRAM. All students attending high school participate in the Youth Skills programs. The 10-session program is designed to provide youth with the skills and information to avoid substance use and make a healthy transition into adulthood. The program, to be implemented by an instructor with the assistance of Operation Snowball participants, includes the following topics: (a) introduction; (b) coping with adolescence; (c) skills for life; (d) communication; (e) decision making; (f) building self-esteem; (g) the facts about drugs; (h) recognizing pressures to use drugs; (i) resisting peer pressure; and (j) overview and future goals. The program promotes participation in the Operation Snowball extra-curricular program and other activities that reinforce the positive, drug-free aspects of their lives.

AWARENESS DAY. Operation Snowball staff and participants often coordinate a day-long event within the high school. The event consists of a presentation to all high school students, parents, and community members. The presentation is similar to those presented at the junior high schools as described on p. 33, and focuses on: (a) resisting peer pressure to use substances; (b) communicating with parents, (c) making decisions and setting goals, and (d) social interactions. The goal of the presentation is to enable Operation Snowball participants to provide positive role modeling and problem-solving skills to nonparticipants. The awareness day also includes an information exchange, where students can visit a central room in the school to discuss drug-related issues with community members (e.g., police officers and counselers) and collect resource materials relating to substance use.

DRUG FREE DANCES. Several drug-free dances are held at the high school over the course of the school year. The dances are planned at the weekly followup meetings and are open to any student in the high school. The dances are held at the high school and are chaperoned by Operation Snowball staff and parents. The Operation Snowball participants are responsible for publicizing the events and coordinating the necessary administrative and entertainment components of the dances. This activity seeks to raise awareness about the Operation Snowball program within the school and provide an alternative to drug and alcohol usage.

FIVE KILOMETER RACE. A five kilometer race is also planned at the weekly followup meetings and is open to any student in the junior high school and high school, parents, teachers, and community members. Student and community members publicize the event, register entries, and coordinate the necessary administrative and medical services on the day of the race. This activity seeks to enlist all of the social networks of the Operation Snowball participants, raise awareness about the program, and provide a health-promoting alternative to drug use.

OPERATION SNOWFLAKES. Although Operation Snowball occurs at the high school level, Operation Snowflake is designed for the junior high school level. Operation Snowflakes are day-long workshops held at the junior high schools, organized and implemented by the adult staff and Operation Snowball participants. The one-day programs typically follow the same basic structure as the Operation Snowball programs (i.e., general and small group sessions and a variety of recreational activities). The general sessions are presented by the Operation Snowball staff members and all of the seventh and eighth grade students. After each general session, the students are divided into smaller groups led by a team of two adult staff members and four Operation Snowball participants.

JUNIOR HIGH SCHOOL PRESENTATIONS. The Operation Snowball staff and participants also coordinate presentations for all junior high school students throughout the school year. Each presentation includes a series of informative skits that typically focus on (a) resisting peer pressure to use substances, (b) communicating with parents, (c) making decisions and setting goals, and (d) social interactions. The goal of these presentations is to enable the high school participants to provide role modeling and problem-solving skills to the students in the junior high schools.

Taken together, the Youth Skills curriculum and the follow up events are the primary means by which the effects of the Operation Snowball programs are expected to generalize to students, teachers, parents, and the community. Operation Snowball is part of an extensive prevention network across Illinois, the Illinois Network to Organize the Understanding of Community Health (InTouch).

InTouch works closely with schools and communities to coordinate a system of community-owned prevention programs, such as Operation Snowball. This facilitates implementation, avoids duplication, and maximizes preventive resources. Overall, Operation Snowball seeks to enlist the support of teachers, parents, and community members to enhance the students' skills and modify the ecological context in which substance usage occurs.

The Operation Snowball program in each community is developed through the efforts of members, school staff, parents, and students. Providing opportunities for students to find meaningful roles in shaping this type of prevention program may increase their commitment to school (Coleman, 1961). In addition, the participants' planning and implementation of the prevention program may increase the likelihood that they will regard the program as their own, and this could deepen their commitment to the program and increase its overall success. The program's emphasis on student, school, and community involvement reduces the reliance on outside resources and enhances the prospects for the program's long-term continuation. By impacting all of the youth's socialization contexts, the program demonstrates ecological sensitivity and increases the likelihood that the skills and behaviors will be expressed, rewarded, and generalized beyond the training session (Bronfenbrenner, 1979; Bandura, 1977). Currently, efforts are underway to evaluate the effectiveness of Operation Snowball. In addition to measuring the adolescent cognitive and behavioral variables, broader school, family, and community indices are being assessed (Rhodes & Jason, 1988).

Limitations of the Community-Based Approach

Despite the inherent appeal of the community-based model, there are several practical and methodological difficulties associated with this approach. The inclusion of many variables (e.g., family, community, media, school system) can limit the researcher's ability to fully assess all of the factors that may be contributing to the final outcome. In addition, the unique ways in which each community actually adapts and implements the program may limit researchers' abilities to make meaningful comparisons across programs. For obvious reasons, gaining control of and fully assessing the influence of all of the variables in a comprehensive community-based approach is an extremely difficult task.

In addition, the reliance on community members, teachers, and peers to design and implement community-based programs can produce profound variation among programs. Not every school district or community implements a program exactly as recommended, increasing the possibility for variation from one community to the next.

Such variation creates difficulties in drawing conclusions about the overall effectiveness and generalizability of a community-based program. In addition, community-based programs that include skills components are plagued with several of the same methodological and practical limitations of the skills-based programs. The methodological difficulties (e.g., reliably measuring substance usage, attrition, unit of analysis) are the same, if not worse, within the context of the broader community. The practical difficulties (e.g., complexity, dissemination) are also present in community-based programs that include skills components.

A Final Word about Community-Based Programs

It is possible that the limitations and complexities discussed above may be contributing to the relative dearth of researchers currently working on more broad-scale, comprehensive community interventions. This is unfortunate, given the enormous potential of this approach.

Community-based programs seek to blend the knowledge of the mental health professional with the strengths and needs of the school and community participants. In Operation Snowball, as in other community-based programs, participants are encouraged to become active owners of both the process and the content of the program (Kelly, Munoz, & Snowden, 1979). By working with the community at all stages of the prevention process, the programs influence not only the youth but their schools and communities. Participants become empowered, resources remain within the community, and behaviors and skills are more likely to be maintained beyond the classroom setting. We view comprehensive community-based prevention programs as the next logical step in the development of substance abuse prevention programs for adolescents.

For readers interested in more information on implementing and evaluating community-based substance abuse prevention programs, several resources are available, including the National Institute on Drug Abuse's Prevention Evaluations Guideline (French, Kaufman, & Burns, 1979), which provides a discussion of community-based programming. Kelly (1987) provides important criteria for conducting research in community settings. Lau, Kane, Berry, Ware, and Roy (1980) offer useful guidelines for evaluations of televised health campaigns, and Biglan and Ary (1985) make several recommendations for enhancing the validity of community-based evaluations.

Chapter 4

Identifying and Referring High-Risk Youth

Since 1980, researchers from DePaul University have conducted substance abuse prevention programs in Chicago. Our twelve-week program provides skills training to seventh and eighth graders, as well as extensive opportunities for role playing. Each year, as we implement the program, we notice huge variations among the students' reactions to the program. Although most youngsters talk to us about their ability to successfully resist peer pressures, several others flaunt their drug usage, registering sly looks of amusement and satisfaction when certain drugs are discussed. Is it possible to provide appropriate prevention services to students with such diverse interests? Can we work with students at lower risk for substance abuse, and at the same time adequately address the needs of those already engaging in problematic usage? Our experiences suggest that whereas the primary prevention programs reviewed in chapter 3 are appropriate for most young people, it may be necessary to provide more intensive and differentiated interventions for those students at higher risk for developing chronic patterns of substance abuse.

But how are we to identify the high-risk youth and refer them to interventions that would most suit their needs? In the following sections, we will review some of the ways in which children are identified as being at risk for substance abuse, including (a) multiple gating, (b) the legal system, and (c) the mental health system. Later in this chapter, we will review the various treatment services available to high risk youth, and we will provide guidelines for referring such youngsters to treatment programs.

IDENTIFYING YOUTH AT HIGH RISK

The early identification of children who will later evidence chronic substance abuse is a particularly challenging task. Despite the prevalence of substance use among youth, a much smaller percentage of youth actually develop patterns of heavy usage and abuse. For example, only 25% of all children who initiate drug

36

use continue after age 23 (Yamaguchi & Kandle, 1984). The key question is whether it is possible to identify those children who will later abuse substances.

In a review of longitudinal studies on antisocial and delinquent behavior, Loeber (1982) emphasized the following patterns, which are indicative of such continuity: (a) the more frequent the problem behavior is, the more stable it tends to be; (b) if the antisocial behavior is noted in more than one setting, it tends to be more stable over time than when it is only noted in one setting; (c) the more varied the types of antisocial behavior a child displays, the more likely it is that these behaviors will persist over time; and (d) the earlier the antisocial pattern becomes evident, the more likely that it will become stable. Thus, children that are identified as likely to chronically abuse substances later should be identified in terms of the following variables: frequency, variety, and seriousness of substance use, age of onset, and the number of settings in which high risk behaviors tend to occur.

Multiple Gating

The multiple gating strategy was developed as a less expensive method of selecting high-risk children among all youth in a particular setting (Loeber & Dishion, 1987). This technique begins with the least expensive screening procedure on all students, and later applies more expensive measures on the high-risk group. Rather than relying on expensive, highly trained professionals to conduct all assessments, the multiple gating procedure uses less expensive procedures (teacher and parent reports) during the initial phases of the assessment.

Based on the risk factors reviewed in earlier chapters, the multiple gating method has been slightly modified for our purposes, to assist in the identification of those youth at highest risk for substance abuse. The two gates used in this assessment effort are presented in Table 4.1 in a general format.

At the first gate, teacher ratings are used to identify those youth who evidence behaviors correlated with substance abuse (i.e. low academic performance, absenteeism, behavior problems in school). High risk children are those who receive at least four checks and/or those who receive a check mark for item 9. Instead of screening the whole class again with another measure, only the high-risk group is reassessed. This time, parents of those high-risk students are interviewed, in order to assess the parents' perceptions of their children's usage patterns, level of conflict with parents, and discipline problems. High risk children are those who receive at least three checks and/or those who receive a check mark for item six. These two gates can lead to the identification of those children who are actively using drugs or whose problem behaviors correlate with drug-taking tendencies.

PSA—D

Table 4.1. Multiple Gating Scales

Scale 1: Teacher Scale

Your school system, in collaboration with (name of consultant), is attempting to identify students that may be at risk for developing patterns of drug usage. Our hope is that if we can identify and intervene with these high risk youth at an early stage, we can interrupt emerging patterns of substance abuse. To accomplish this goal, we are asking for the assistance of teachers in identifying students who may be using drugs or at risk for using and abusing drugs. For each statement listed, check the responses that describe each of your students. Thank you for your assistance.

....Student's Name

Please check those items that are true for the student mentioned above.

_____ 1. It is likely that (he/she) smokes cigarettes.
_____ 2. It is likely that (he/she) drinks alcohol.
_____ 3. It is likely that (he/she) smokes marijuana.
_____ 4. It is likely that (he/she) uses other illegal drugs.
_____ 5. Student generally exhibits low academic performance.
_____ 6. (He/she) is absent more often than most other students.
_____ 7. I frequently have to take disciplinary actions in response to (his/her) behavior in school.
_____ 8. (He/she) has difficulty making friends and successfully interacting with other students and teachers.
_____ 9. I feel that (he/she) probably has a drug problem.

Scale 2: PARENT SCALE (to be administered over the telephone)

Your child's school system, in collaboration with (name of consultant), is attempting to identify students that may be most at risk for developing patterns of drug usage. Our hope is that if we can identify and intervene with these high risk youth at an early stage, we can interrupt emerging patterns of substance abuse. To accomplish this goal, we are asking for the assistance of parents in identifying youngsters who may be using drugs or at risk for using and abusing drugs. This telephone survey should take no longer than five minutes. Any information that you make available to us will be kept confidential. Your participation in this survey is voluntary, and you are encouraged to ask questions now or at any point in our conversation. Do you agree to participate?

For each statement, indicate, (by saying true or false), whether or not a statement applies to you and/or your child.

_____ 1. I have difficulties setting limits with my child.
_____ 2. My child and I get into frequent arguments.
_____ 3. My child frequently resists going to school.

_____ 4. I am concerned that my child may be associating with drug using peers.

_____ 5. My child has difficulty making friends and successfully interacting with friends and adults.

_____ 6. I am concerned that my child may have a drug problem.

Given that these questionnaires are not a regular component of the school, and may raise the concerns of parents, it will be important to obtain consent before they are administered.

The Legal System

High-risk teenagers are often identified and referred to treatment through the juvenile justice system. Chronic juvenile offenders and those brought to the attention of the police, for behaviors such as theft or drunken driving, are often at risk for substance abuse. These youth are frequently referred to drug treatment centers as an alternative or an adjunct to a legal intervention. For example, frequently the penalty for adolescent offenders that have been identified as driving while under the influence of alcohol is attendance at Alcoholics Anonymous or related treatment programs. Identification and referral to intervention through this process can interrupt emerging patterns of alcoholism or drug abuse.

The Mental Health System

Youthful substance abusers are sometimes identified and referred to the mental health system. Such youth may be brought into family or individual treatment for problem behaviors at school or at home. The academic difficulties or problematic relationships that are identified as the presenting problems, however, are frequently related to underlying patterns of substance abuse. Rather than treating these problems within traditional settings, many mental health professionals refer adolescent substance abusers to specialized treatment services.

REFERRING YOUTH TO TREATMENT

We have identified some of the pathways through which high-risk youth are identified and referred to treatment. It is important to note, however, that many young drug users may not perceive that their usage is a problem. Such youngsters will not be motivated to seek help with what others have identified as a problem, particularly when their peer culture supports these health-compromising behaviors. In addition, parents are sometimes reluctant to refer their high-risk youngsters to treatment, because of the stigma associated with drug abuse (Shapiro, 1985). To complicate matters, personnel are frequently unsure about how to handle the high risk adolescents who come to their attention. These are

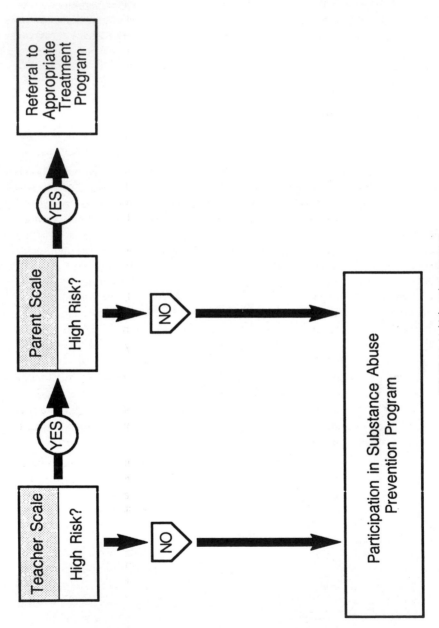

FIGURE 4.1. Multiple gating sequence.

difficult problems and there are no simple solutions. Not only should youngsters be treated with kindness and respect, but a good deal of emotional support and reassurance should be provided. The early contacts with the treatment facility will set the tone for the rest of the treatment. If youngsters feel that their needs are being met at the setting, it is less likely that they will resist treatment or terminate prematurely. Therefore, knowledge of the range of treatment facilities available to meet the needs of high-risk youth is often the first step in helping these youngsters. Our next section will review this topic.

Selection of Treatment Services

In the following sections, we will review some of the early intervention and treatment services available for adolescents at high risk for substance abuse. This review should facilitate the ability of practitioners to appropriately refer youth that have been identified as needing substance abuse treatment. Adolescents engaging in heavy use or in danger of developing patterns of chronic substance abuse can be treated in one's private practice, in outpatient clinics, non-hospital residential settings, or hospitals.

The selection of an appropriate intervention depends on the severity of the drug problem, the types of drugs being used and abused, the physical and mental health of the youth, and the adequacy of the support system (e.g., home environment, family relationships, involvement in school, peer relationships, employment situation) (Friedman, 1985a). When youth are identified as being at high risk on the basis of the multiple gating procedures, much of the referral information needed in order to make a referral has already been obtained. For example, data from the scales and behavioral assessment provide information concerning the youth's home environment, family and peer relations, and school adjustment.

With this information, high-risk children can be referred to (a) hospital detoxification programs, (b) residential programs, or (c) outpatient programs. Each of these types of programs will be reviewed below.

HOSPITAL DETOXIFICATION PROGRAMS. These are for youngsters who are at serious medical risk due to overdose, or who are at risk of physical withdrawal symptoms. These youngsters typically have histories of long-term, heavy use of addictive drugs, and may require detoxification in a controlled medical environment for medical or more severe psychiatric problems.

RESIDENTIAL (NON-HOSPITAL) PROGRAMS. These programs may be required for heavy drug users who need a 24-hour structured program and a controlled environment. These are non-medical residential centers that provide intensive structure and supervision. Most of these youngsters' homes lack structure and supports, and many of the adolescents lack motivation and self-control.

OUTPATIENT PROGRAMS. Close to 80% of all youthful substance abusers are referred to and treated at outpatient settings. The majority of adolescent substance abusers, those that have adequate support systems in the community and do not have underlying psychiatric or medical problems, are safely treated in an outpatient setting. These programs use three primary psychotherapy modalities, (i.e., individual, family, and group therapy) and the treatments often incorporate various theoretical approaches (e.g., reality, gestalt, behavioral).

These programs provide short- and long-term treatment and supportive services, or else act as referral centers to agencies offering a wide array of services. Some programs also operate day school programs for adolescents who have dropped out of school (Friedman & Beschner, 1985).

In the next section, we will provide an overview of treatment modalities typically used in these settings, as well as an in-depth examination of a Chicago-based outpatient setting.

OUTPATIENT TREATMENT MODALITIES
FOR ADOLESCENT DRUG ABUSERS

In a survey of 70 adolescent outpatient drug treatment programs across the country, it was found that 68% of the staff time was devoted to drug abuse counseling (Friedman & Beschner, 1985). Approximately 50% of counseling time was devoted to individual therapy and the remainder to group and family therapy. We will review these different types of treatment approaches. More detailed sources of information on these treatment approaches are available (Marks, Darhoff, & Granick, 1985; Friedman & Beschner, 1985). In addition, the National Institute On Drug Abuse (French et al., 1979) has published a useful overview of treatment services for adolescent substance abusers, as well as a monograph devoted to current research in the area of drug abuse treatment (Harris, 1985).

Individual Therapy

In certain situations, individual counseling is preferred over group or family therapy (Marks et al., 1985). For example, some adolescents may feel that they need complete confidentiality regarding the issues discussed in treatment. These adolescents may be highly anxious, or may have severe difficulties getting along with family members. Within individual treatment, reality, gestalt, and behavioral therapy are frequently employed.

Reality Therapy. Reality therapy is the most commonly used approach when treating adolescent substance abusers. This approach, developed by William Glasser in the 1950s and 1960s, is based on the assumption that individuals are responsible for what they do. As the therapists establish rapport, children evaluate their behaviors and gain more responsibility and maturity. For readers interested in a more in-depth look at this approach, Glasser (1985) provides an excellent overview of the theoretical basis and applications of reality therapy. In an earlier publication, Glasser (1969) applies the concepts of reality therapy to adolescent problem behaviors and school settings.

To date, two studies have examined the use of reality therapy as a treatment approach for adolescent drug and/or alcohol abusers (Wunderlich, Lozes, & Lewis, 1974; Bratter, 1973). Unfortunately, methodological shortcomings in these studies limit our ability to draw conclusions about the effectiveness of reality therapy.

Gestalt Therapy. Gestalt therapy was founded by Frederick S. Perls and Laura Perls in the 1940s. This approach teaches youngsters to pay more attention to their immediate experiences and to be more direct and open in their communications (Simkin & Yontef, 1985). Gestalt therapy aims at helping youngsters express painful emotions as a means of resolving conflict and improving difficult interpersonal relationships. Readers seeking more information on this approach might consult Simkin and Yontef (1985) and Perls (1976).

In a recent evaluation of treatment approaches, Friedman (1985a) found that Gestalt therapy showed a statistically significant treatment outcome. Until more research is conducted with this approach, however, we can not draw conclusions concerning the effectiveness of this approach.

Behavior Therapy. Behavior therapy has been defined as the application of classical and operant conditioning modelling and cognitive restructuring principles to the treatment of clinical problems (Wilson, 1985). Behavior therapy today is marked by a diversity of experimentally derived procedures (Kazdin & Wilson, 1978).

From a behavioral perspective, substance abuse is a learned behavior. Learning can occur through classical conditioning (e.g., drug usage occurring at a video store in the community is paired or associated with an adolescent beginning to experiment with substances), operant conditioning (e.g., friends reward the youngster for substance usage), modeling (e.g., observing parents or siblings using substances), or cognitive restructuring (e.g., an adolescent says "if others experiment with drugs, then it is acceptable for me to also experiment with drugs") (Stumphauzer, 1980). Behavioral approaches that have been used to treat adolescent substance abuse include: (a) counterconditioning, using aversive imagery in combination with the drug behavior (Kolvin, 1967); (b) systematic desensitization, imagining and successfully dealing with progressively more stressful events that may lead to drug use (Kraft, 1970); (c) contingent reinforcement, rewards for abstaining and punishment for usage (Stybel, 1977); and (d) contingency contracting, wherein the adolescent and parent establish consequences for drug use and more prosocial alternatives (Cook & Petersen, 1985). Stitzer, Bigelow, and McCaul (1985) provide an excellent review of the procedures involved in the behavioral treatment of adolescent substance abuse.

Evaluations of these approaches provide support for use of behavior therapy procedures with adolescent substance abusers. Methodological shortcomings, however, including the reliance on self-reports and small samples, limit the ability to draw more firm conclusions about the effectiveness of this approach.

Family Therapy

Several recent family treatment outcome studies with substance abusers have demonstrated the efficacy of family therapy in improving family functioning and decreasing drug abuse in family members (Lewis, Filsinger, Conger, & McAvoy, 1981; Lewis & McAvoy, 1983; Stanton & Todd, 1982; Szapocznik, Kurtivnes, Foote, Perez-Vidal & Hervis, 1983; 1986). In one of the best controlled family therapy studies, Stanton and Todd (1982) found that structural-strategic family therapy with young adult heroin abusers not only improved the family decision making and conflict resolution skills, but significantly decreased the drug use.

Structural-strategic family therapy is one of the most commonly used family therapy approaches employed by family-oriented drug abuse treatment programs (Cole & Davis, 1978). The model is rooted in the work of Salvador Minuchin (1974) and the strategic family therapy approach developed by Jay Haley (1976, 1980, 1984). Stanton and Todd (1982) were the first family therapists to demonstrate the utility of integrating structural and strategic therapies when working with drug-abusing families. Their model consists of four stages of treatment, including: (1) creating a context for change; (2) establishing treatment goals; (3) challenging the family structure, belief systems, and transactional patterns; and (4) consolidating changes. (See Fishman, Stanton, & Rosman, 1982 and Piercy & Frankel, 1986 for more comprehensive overviews of the major concepts and treatment strategies of the structural-strategic family therapy approach with adolescent substance abusers).

Group Therapy

There are many advantages of using group therapy in place of, or as an adjunct to, individual or family therapy. The social stress model posits that youth who have a limited repertoire of interpersonal skills and inadequate social support networks are at risk for substance abuse. Group therapy provides opportunities for peer involvement and interaction, enabling adolescents to practice important social skills (Licarione, 1985). Peer support groups can decrease the feelings of alienation characteristic of many adolescent substance abusers. Support in these groups can provide members with a sense of belonging and confidence, and these positive feelings can have facilitating effects in interactions outside of therapy with family and friends. Licarione (1985) provides a detailed overview of the various group approaches involved in treating adolescent substance abusers.

In situations where the adolescent substance abuser refuses to participate in group therapy or other forms of treatment, it may be most advantageous to intervene at the parental level through the use of a parenting group. By coaching patients to engage in different behaviors with their adolescents, the drug abusing youth can be indirectly impacted. Two parenting group approaches that have demonstrated effectiveness with an adolescent substance abuse population are: (1) Strategic parenting and (2) Training in parenting skills.

The Strategic Parenting group approach (Efron & Rowe, 1987) is designed to teach parents family systems theory and strategic therapy principles and techniques.

The Training in Parenting Skills (TIPS) model provides information to parents about addictive drugs, the effects of these drugs, and the methods that family members can use to eliminate drug use.

Northwest Youth Outreach

Northwest Youth Outreach started in 1959 as a YMCA-sponsored social program, designed for youth in the northwest side of Chicago (reviewed in Kusnetz, 1985). This outreach and outpatient program now provides services to approximately 900 outpatient clients (75% white, 15% Hispanic, 10% Black). In addition, approximately 12,000 young people receive indirect services through the school and community outreach efforts. Because preventive approaches have been covered in other chapters in this book, we will focus on the outpatient component. Northwest Outreach staff report that alcohol and marijuana, in combination, are the primary drugs of abuse on the part of 75% of the clients. Other widely used drugs include hallucinogens, amphetamines, cocaine, and PCP.

Referral Sources. Clients in the Northwest Youth Outreach program are primarily recruited from an outreach effort conducted in the community. Northwest Outreach staff spend a portion of their day where youngsters hang out, such as schoolyards, street corners, and parks. When a particular youngster is identified as having a drug problem, the outreach worker forms a relationship with that youngster and works toward moving the youngster into the formal treatment service. Other adolescents enter the program by referrals from schools, parents, and community agencies (i.e., the police, juvenile justice system, mental health agencies).

Fee Structure. The Northwest Outreach program is supported primarily by public funds, 80% of the operating budget comes from the state, and 10% from the municipality. An additional 10% is supplied by private sources, such as the United Way. No fees are charged for participation in the program, but families are asked for voluntary donations.

Treatment Program. Approximately 70% of the youngsters in the formal treatment program participate in group therapy. Family therapy is also recommended for all clients, and at any one time 20% are involved in this treatment approach. All youngsters are required to participate in individual therapy, and 70% also participate in recreational activities. Typically, a youngster spends 30–36 weeks in the formal program, with an additional 4–6 months of aftercare.

The treatment program has four levels. In Level one (6 to 12 weeks), the youngster is assessed and family members are interviewed. The youngster then begins individual counseling and is enrolled in educational classes. The youngster next moves to Level two, the abstinence phase. During this phase, the youngster is encouraged to participate in self-help groups (e.g., Alcoholics Anonymous, Narcotics Anonymous), and parents are encouraged to attend their own self-help groups modeled after Tough Love or Families Anonymous. In Level three, the program focuses on enhancing coping skills (e.g., decisionmaking, communication, setting goals). The youngster also participates as a leader of a self-help group, in order to serve as a role model for those youngsters at a more beginning phase of treatment. Level four is the aftercare phase, at which time the youth attends followup meetings at an after care support group. If at any time during the program adolescents relapse or drop out, they are actively encouraged to reenter at a lower level.

Intensive Outpatient Treatment Program. Northwest Youth Outreach also offers an intensive outpatient program for youth who are having difficulty remaining abstinent in the regular treatment program. This is a highly structured, after-school program. Youth are expected to participate in individual, family, and group therapies on a weekly basis for a minimum of twelve hours per week. The intensive outpatient program was specifically designed to prevent expensive relapse and more intensive treatment.

Evaluation. Although a rigorous evaluation has not yet been conducted of the short- and long-term effectiveness of the various program components, internal data indicate that between 35% to 40% of those who begin the program complete the four treatment levels. Unfortunately, as with most programs of this nature, evaluation is typically not done or is conducted in a rather imprecise manner.

A Final Word on Referrals

Regardless of whether a youth is being referred to a hospital, a residential program, or an outpatient treatment center, those making the referrals need to carefully check all admission criteria of a particular program. There are frequently age, gender, or geographic restrictions. In addition, some programs will not accept children with certain types of legal problems or drug usage patterns. Other programs will only consider youth whose families can afford the treatment fees.

Most programs are small and accept youngsters only from their local communities. Indeed, the decision as to which program is chosen is often based on geographic factors. Outside of major urban areas, there are currently few programs from which to choose (Friedman, 1985b).

As we suggested earlier, in attempting to locate an appropriate program for a youngster one must first consider the types of problems the adolescent is experiencing, the severity of the drug problem, the adjustment and motivation of the youth, the family functioning, and the community support systems. The multiple gating process reviewed in this chapter will facilitate the identification of high-risk youth, and, to a large extent, provide the basis for appropriate referral.

Of course, intervention programs need not be limited to those specifically focused on drug abuse. They can include any services or activities that interrupt emerging patterns of substance abuse by strengthening prosocial peer relationships, improving parent–child communication and alliances, and enhancing interpersonal skills for dealing with stress. For example, scouts, 4-H clubs, athletic leagues, and other organized community programs can provide youth with opportunities to successfully interact with other youth and adults. Most communities have services and educational agencies that can play important roles in this respect. As we pointed out in chapter 2, the risk for substance abuse is frequently offset by the ability of youth to cope with many life stressors and challenges. To the extent that we can identify those at highest risk for substance abuse at an early age and refer them to the appropriate intervention, we may be able to prevent the development of chronic, health-endangering patterns of abuse.

Chapter 5

Prevention Program Guidelines

In the previous chapters, we have provided a framework for a better understanding of current efforts designed to reduce and prevent substance abuse among children and adolescents. This chapter offers practical guidelines and a process for translating the theory and strategies into effective action. Many of the techniques and processes we will be discussing have emerged from our experiences in designing and implementing substance abuse prevention programs within Illinois' school systems. The guidelines should assist readers in their efforts to implement drug abuse programs. Although this discussion will focus largely on issues related to initiating, implementing, and evaluating school-based programs, many of the guidelines and processes that we will be reviewing are applicable to community or clinic-based settings.

As anyone who has consulted with an agency or school system is well aware, providing intervention services is a complex activity, and there are many factors that affect success. Both subtle and not so-subtle-variables can facilitate or impede a consultant's success within the setting. For example, a board of education that asks a consultant to implement a prevention program may, in fact, be reluctant to provide the necessary time and support for such an action, and thus may actively oppose all efforts needed to ensure the program's success. Examples of subtle sabotage include repeated scheduling difficulties or lack of support from key teachers and staff. Under such circumstances, even the most carefully designed prevention program may not have a chance. Therefore, mental health consultants must not only have the resources to implement and evaluate appropriate programs, but must be skilled at assessing the interest of key administrators, understanding the power conflicts that might exist among school officials, and gaining the trust and support of the administration.

In the following sections, we will be reviewing several stages in the process of consulting to a school or agency including: (a) entering the setting, (b) identifying and defining goals, (c) implementing the substance abuse prevention program, and (d) evaluating the intervention (see Figure 5.1).

STAGE ONE: ENTRY

Regardless of whether he or she is a school employee or an outside consultant, the person setting up the prevention service may initially be perceived as intrusive. The mere presence of the consultant could indicate that change is about to occur, and this may raise doubts and defensiveness among the staff. Under such conditions, the consultant first needs to gain the acceptance of key personnel within the system (Parsons & Meyers, 1985).

To facilitate this process, the consultant needs to be able to identify sources of resistance. Take our earlier example: members of the board of education, having hired a consultant, may actually be resistant to change. Systems tend to seek a state of equilibrium, and a program may be seen as a possible drain on resources and thus a threat to the stability of the system. Active attempts need to be made to reduce or minimize the threat of instability. This can be accomplished by careful observance of existing policies and regularities (e.g., if certain classes are perceived as central to a child's education, be sure not to remove children from those classes when the program is being implemented). Respecting the value of key administrators and professionals will also do much to smooth the entry process (Parsons & Meyers, 1985). Generally, the less change requested, the less resistance the consultant will encounter, and thus the more quickly acceptance will occur for the overall plan. In this context, it is better initially to forgo complex, setting-disruptive plans and, instead, adopt less intrusive plans that can later evolve closer to one's ideal. As the setting gains trust in the consultant, the school officials will provide the program with more resources and options.

Our own experiences as consultants to an Illinois substance abuse prevention agency illustrate this process. In our initial role as consultants, we provided assistance in evaluating their statewide system — a community-based substance abuse program called Operation Snowball. (See chapter 3 for a description of this program.) Throughout the early stages of this consultation process, we worked closely with key individuals, established a good rapport with agency officials, and emphasized their importance in the evaluation process. Over the course of our work within this agency, it soon became clear that this agency, as is characteristic of most agencies, did have internal struggles for power and some resistance to change.

Although the Operation Snowball program had been in existence for over ten years, the agency had never conducted a rigorous evaluation of the programs' effectiveness. In order to gain support, we attended numerous board meetings where agency members and volunteers were given the opportunity to make suggestions and ask questions concerning the evaluation strategy. Over a four

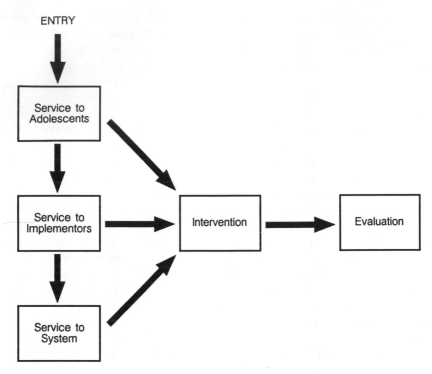

FIGURE 5.1. Consultation flow chart. A version of this flow chart appeared in Parsons, R.D., & Meyers, J. (1985). *Developing consultation skills*. San Francisco: Jossey-Bass Publishers.

month period, through a steady process of collaboration and information gathering, we earned the trust and acceptance of agency personnel. The staff members began to share with us their frustrations over the variation among programs across the state. Some schools had developed comprehensive, community-based programs; others were less comprehensive and lacked any program guidelines. The result was an inconsistent delivery of substance abuse preventive services to youth across Illinois. Given this variation among chapters, we decided not to attempt an overall evaluation of the Operation Snowball program. Instead, it appeared that a more appropriate strategy would be to assist in the development, dissemination, and evaluation of systematic program guidelines. Because we had established a positive collaborative relationship with the key agency personnel, when we did present our intervention plans, they were unanimously accepted by the Board of Operation Snowball. If, however, we had suggested these large-scale modifications at an earlier stage, it is likely that our suggestions would not have been supported.

As has been stated, a crucial element in gaining acceptance in a school system involves establishing a positive relationship with individuals serving as the "gatekeepers." Gatekeepers — such as the principal, guidance counselors, and certain teachers — oversee the consultant's entry into the agency or school. Some have been assigned this role formally, others more informally. In fact, if all initial negotiations occur with only the senior administrative personnel, this may signal an alignment or coalition that might later be alienating when trying to work with the other staff members (Glidewell, 1959). It is critical to find out where the real power and decisionmaking resides. If a teacher who has been in the system for a long time, one who has considerable support among other teachers, opposes the intervention, it may fail even if the principal is supportive.

In addition to understanding the internal power structures, the consultant should be familiar with those factors somewhat external to the school that may have a significant impact on its functioning (Caplan, 1970). One example is the board of education, which is associated with many schools, and which approves decisions about personnel, budgets, and professional philosophy. Neighborhood and community groups can also have a significant impact on preventive initiatives, as can churches, local and state policies, and government agencies. These forces can influence the goals and philosophy of the school as well as its structure and internal dynamics. For example, if the school board imposes a shift in education to a "back to basics" approach, a proposed substance abuse prevention program may be cut to provide additional time for implementing more basic curricula.

The consultant should also be familiar with past historic issues which have confronted the school or community setting. If, in the past, many other practitioners who have tried and failed to implement a prevention program in the school, the staff might be more negative, cautious, and reluctant to attempt another intervention.

STAGE TWO: GOAL IDENTIFICATION AND DEFINITION

Throughout this stage, the consultant collaborates with the staff to identify goals and to determine which goals of the setting are to be worked on. There are several possible levels of consultation: working with the staff to help them implement programs, directly implementing services, or jointly working with the staff and community members in implementing the programs.

When implementing Operation Snowball, for example, a consultant could work at various levels, and in our actual work we have done this. For example, the consultant could implement and evaluate an Operation Snowball program within a school system (i.e., direct service to the students). Alternatively, the consultant could hold workshops that provide guidelines for implementation and evaluation to the Operation Snowball staff members (i.e., service to program implementors). Finally, the consultant could collaborate with program staff and community members, to develop implementation and evaluation guidelines that could be taught to all Operation Snowball staff. At this level, the consultant is indirectly impacting the entire system.

In view of the prevention goals — reaching the largest number of people — the consultant might consider more system-oriented objectives. Although we prefer this higher level, practical demands require that the consultant recognize the perceived needs and use this framework to do what is possible given the constraints of the setting. Therefore, when identifying goals, a consultant should work at the highest possible level of entry acceptable to the setting, even when this level might be less than ideal (Parsons & Meyers, 1985).

STAGE THREE: INTERVENTION

At the third stage, specific intervention strategies are selected, developed, or implemented. The intervention, in a sense, has begun even during the early contacts. For example, when goals are identified, the staff might feel a sense of relief, and these early attitudes and feelings can effect an intervention. The relationships established at this early point will have potent effects on the integrity and success of the later intervention (Parsons & Meyers, 1985).

Of course, the consultant needs to have specific knowledge and expertise in the various areas of intervention (e.g., drug education, skills-based curricula, community-based programs). We recommend that intervention strategies be selected and implemented in a cooperative manner. Even though the consultant is expected to provide answers to diverse issues, interventions with the greatest chance of being accepted by the setting are those developed jointly by the consultant and staff members (Kelly et al., 1979). Accordingly, the consultant needs to encourage the staff to provide suggestions as to how the program might be implemented and to have the freedom to reject consultant ideas that seem impractical or not good "fits" with the setting (Parsons & Meyers, 1985). In this way, the staff members are empowered and feel that they are essential contributors to "their" intervention.

In the following sections, we will present a substance abuse prevention curriculum for grades six through eight, to be offered as the main component of a substance abuse prevention class or as the skills component of a more community-based program. This description should provide the reader with a better sense of how skills training programs are organized and implemented. The curriculum is designed to provide a general framework that can be modified to fit school or community-based programs. (References to resources and material that may be useful in modifying this curricula, as well as information relating to other available skills-based curricula, are provided in Appendix A.)

The course was derived from the Operation Snowball skills curricula, the work of Spivack and Shure (1979), and related skills-based programs. It consists of ten sessions and two evaluation components. Each of the forty-five-minute sessions contain a variety of classroom activities, including discussions, role playing, and homework assignments. All of the materials to complete each activity, including step-by-step instructions, are provided in the text and appendix. The sessions include:

1. Introduction
2. Understanding adolescence
3. Skills for life
4. Building self-esteem
5. Communication skills
6. Decisionmaking
7. Substances
8. Identifying pressures to use drugs
9. Resisting peer pressure
10. Overview and future goals.

Before introducing the curriculum, we will briefly address some of the general issues and concerns that the practitioner should be sensitive to when implementing a skills-based program. These general areas include: (a) establishing rapport, (b) setting rules, (c) facilitating role plays, (d) enhancing assignment compliance, and (e) obtaining consent.

Establishing Rapport

Given the emphasis on interpersonal behaviors and values, an accepting classroom environment and good rapport with the students is essential. We have found that a good way to establish rapport with the adolescents is to actively participate in the activities. The consultant or leader can facilitate open communication through self-disclosure and modeling of cooperative behaviors during the sessions.

Setting Rules

Skills-based programs are designed to involve students actively. Students are asked to talk about themselves and to practice ways of interacting with others; they are encouraged to share their feelings and experiences and to raise any questions that they have. Thus, it is important to establish certain rules to facilitate acceptance and communication. Some of these rules may include: listening to others, respecting confidentiality, and not interrupting. Although most students will follow the classroom rules and actively participate in the activities and discussions, some may have difficulties with the rules. For example, a student may repeatedly interrupt or ridicule group members when they are discussing sensitive issues. This may be an indication that the young person feels uneasy with the

PSA—E

topics being discussed. It may be necessary to meet with the student individually to discuss these disruptive behaviors and to assess the possible presence of underlying substance abuse or related problem behaviors.

Another type of problem, which on the surface appears to be minor but could upset many key individuals within a school, concerns the noise level. Most programs are designed to encourage discussion and activity and the noise level may be above what is customary. A certain amount of noise is to be expected when students interact, and it is not counterproductive. If the noise level does become excessive, it is important to request that every one talk more quietly.

Facilitating Role Plays

Some of the activities in the curriculum require role playing, in which students are given the opportunity to practice the skills in class so that they will be prepared to refuse drugs outside of class. In facilitating role plays, the leader's job is to provide encouragement to students when they practice resistance skills and to elicit appropriate feedback from the rest of the class. Because feedback from peers helps to shape appropriate resistance skills and promotes class norms against drugs, it is important to involve the entire class in the role play activities.

We have found that role playing is generally the most popular component of our substance abuse prevention programs. It is often best to first model a role play situation in order to give the students an example of what is expected. Try to create an atmosphere of relaxation and fun when assigning a role play. In addition, the instructor should detail the specific tasks for everyone involved in a role play, establish a time limit, and encourage feedback from classmates. Try to allow the role play to continue until the student has had a chance to refuse the drug offer. You may need to cut the action if: (a) a problem develops that interferes with the role play, (b) the role play becomes unrealistic, or (c) the role play is not going anywhere. Students not actively involved in the role play may need instruction in being active observers — watching carefully, listening, not talking, and not making fun of the actors. Tell the audience that their job is to pay attention and to make comments during the discussion that follows.

Assignments

The curriculum includes homework assignments following each session. Often they involve completing work sheets or carrying out a specific behavior. To facilitate homework compliance and encourage family involvement in the prevention program, students should practice skills at home and work with their parents on the homework. We also encourage students to obtain their parents' initials on all completed assignments. With assignments directly involving families, be sensitive to the variety of students' family backgrounds. For example, students from homes with working parents or with high levels of disorganization may find it difficult to involve their families in homework assignments. Be prepared to suggest alternatives, such as completing the assignment with a friend. In addition, the consultant may have more difficulty with homework compliance in settings outside of school (e.g., community centers). Although you need to emphasize the importance of the homework, you should recognize that all children will not complete them. As the program develops, however, it is reasonable to expect higher compliance with homework assignments. Always provide students with either verbal or written feedback on their completed assignments.

Obtaining Consent

Programs that are not a regular component of the school require that written consent be obtained from the participants and parents or guardians. Because students often either forget to take the consent forms home or to return them to class, gaining consent can be difficult and time-consuming. We recommend that you begin the process of gaining consent well in advance of the scheduled pretesting and program implementation. We have designed a consent form (see Table 5.1) that can be adapted to various programs and settings.

YOUTH SKILLS PROGRAM

Pretesting

Goal To ascertain the students' pre-program level of substance usage, knowledge about substances, and skills.

Introduction to Class Explain to the students that they will soon be participating in a Youth Skills course and that you will be asking them to complete some surveys in order to determine the effectiveness of the program. Ask the students to put a code (e.g. their birthdates) on the pretests rather than their names. Emphasize that their answers will remain confidential and that the information will not be used against them in any way.

Activities

● Administer and collect all pretests, review instructions with the class, and answer any questions. (A relevant test for this assessment can be found in Appendix B.)
● If your evaluation includes a control group, administer the pretest to the control group at this time.

INSTRUCTOR'S NOTE: You may wish to include additional measures (e.g., biochemical samples, the bogus pipeline procedure) to promote honest reporting on the pretests. This will depend on various factors including: (a) the intended use of the data, (b) the evaluation budget, and (c) the policies and restrictions of the setting. (See the section on evaluation in this chapter for a discussion of these and other evaluation procedures.)

Dear Parent:

This school year, (name of agency) will be working with the faculty and administration of (name of school or setting) to provide a Youth Skills substance abuse prevention program. This year's program seeks to enhance students' ability to make healthy decisions and to resist the pressures that lead some children to abuse drugs and alcohol. The program, which is free, consists of ten hour-long sessions. Each of the sessions contains a variety of classroom activities including, discussions, role playing, and homework assignments. The program will provide information about the challenges of adolescence and the short- and long-term effects of drug use. The students will be provided with training in the skills necessary to avoid using drugs, including decision making, peer pressure resistance, and goal setting. The program will occur during the students' scheduled health classes and will be implemented by personnel from (name of agency) in collaboration with teachers from (name of school or setting).

Your child's class has been selected to take part in this year's Youth Skills program. At the beginning and end of the program, we will be assessing the children's social and personal skills, drug usage, and knowledge, and attitudes about drugs. This information will be kept confidential, and it will permit us to evaluate the effectiveness of this prevention program. Given this information, I agree to the following:

1. I have freely volunteered to take part in this program.
2. I have been informed in advance as to what I will be doing in the project.
3. I understand that I will have the chance to ask questions and to have my questions answered.
4. I am aware that I have the right to withdraw and not take part at any time.
5. My signature below indicates that I agree to the four statements above.

Student's Signature

Parent/Guardian Permission

I give my child permission to participate in the program described above.

Parent or Guardian

Thank you for your cooperation. If you have any further questions about this program, please feel free to contact (name of consultant) at (name of agency), (telephone number).

Principal's name and signature

FIGURE 5.2. Consent form.

Session One: Introduction to Program

Goal To introduce the goals of the program and to build a supportive classroom.

Introduction to Class Inform the students that the program is designed to help young people learn about themselves and avoid using drugs. Provide a general outline of the program, including a discussion of the main areas to be covered. Inform the students that there will be a discussion of many different issues and concerns about adolescence, and opportunities to learn and practice important life skills. An effort will be made to develop an atmosphere where students feel comfortable discussing topics openly and honestly. In order to accomplish this, students can not repeat the self-disclosures of others to anyone outside of class. To the extent that this rule is followed, feelings of trust will be stronger among class members.

Activities

- Explain to the group that you hope that they will develop an atmosphere in which people act toward one another in supportive ways.
- Develop and post rules for establishing a comfortable and supportive environment.
- Explain that one of the primary activities of the Youth Skills program is skills training. Some of the skills that they will learn and practice include: (a) decision making, (b) communicating, (c) building self-esteem, (d) resisting peer pressure, and (e) setting goals. Discuss the importance of these skills in coping with the challenges of adolescence.

Homework Have the students complete the "Being Supportive" worksheet (see Appendix C) which asks students to imagine ways of giving support to a friend.

INSTRUCTOR'S NOTE: Because many adolescents are threatened by the possibility of rejection or ridicule, it may be difficult to quickly establish a positive, trusting environment. Therefore, it is critical to set a warm and supportive tone for this and subsequent sessions. This can be facilitated by sharing your feelings, reinforcing the expression of open and trusting emotions, and emphasizing the importance of the rules (e.g., confidentiality of all discussions).

Session Two: Understanding Adolescence

Goal To examine the issues and concerns of the teenage years.

Introduction to Class Explain to the class that the focus so far has been on building a safe, supportive classroom atmosphere. The class will now begin examining some of the developmental changes and personal concerns that students are beginning to experience (e.g., physical changes, changing relationships). This course will help students learn more about what it means to experience and cope effectively with adolescence.

Activities

- Briefly review the previous session and explain that throughout the course, the students will be learning about and practicing the skills and ideas discussed in that session.
- Instructors present a discussion about the changes that occur during adolescence. For example, developing friendships with members of the opposite sex and exploring new ways of relating to parents can be both challenging and confusing.
- Facilitate a discussion of the questions and concerns generated by the lecture. For example, you might have the class talk about the concerns that will arise during their teen years (e.g., understanding their own needs and feelings, dealing with friends that want to use drugs, making decisions about sexuality, and setting goals for the future).
- Ask the students to think of at least two people that they can turn to for support when dealing with these concerns. Students might talk with these people when making difficult decisions or dealing with challenging problems.

Homework Have the students complete the "About Me" worksheet (see Appendix D), which provides an outline for students to think about some of their needs and feelings.

INSTRUCTOR'S NOTE: The major goal of this session is to increase the students' awareness of their physical and emotional changes. Such self awareness will sensitize youth to the fact that their feelings of confusion and uncertainty are normal. Some youth in the class will be less developmentally advanced than others, so it will be important to emphasize that not all adolescents change at the same rate.

Session Three: Skills for Life

Goal To help students think about the types of skills that they will need to deal with the challenges they are facing.

Introduction to Class Briefly review the major concepts of the previous unit. Inform the class that today's session will be focusing on important skills, as well as the strengths that they already have, with which to cope with life challenges.

Activites

- Review the concerns that were raised during the Session Two discussion. Lead the class in a discussion that generates some of the skills (e.g., communicating, decision making, goal setting skills) that will be useful in dealing with these concerns.

● Explain to the students that adolescence is a time for acquiring adult skills, exploring options, and taking risks. Instead of learning the skills in a hit-or-miss fashion, this course will systematically teach some of the skills necessary to better cope with the stressors of life.

● Pass out and have students complete the "Shield against Stress" worksheet (see Appendix E). The worksheet asks students to explore some of the skills that they may already possess as well as those they may need to offset the impact of stress.

Homework Have the students complete the "Measuring my Skills" (see Appendix F) worksheet, which provides an outline for students to identify which skills they have and which they need to develop further.

Session Four: Building Self-Esteem

Goal To recognize and share strengths and experiences of success.

Introduction to Class Briefly review the major concepts of the previous unit. Remind the class that the following sessions will focus on developing some of the skills that were previously identified.

Tell students that today's unit will explore the concept of self-esteem, and discover some of the ways we can feel better about ourselves and help others to feel better about themselves. Explain that throughout their teen years, they will be spending considerable time thinking about who they are, what they are good at, and how they are seen by others. All of these things affect their feelings about themselves and whether or not they feel confident. Suggest to the class that because they are changing so fast and trying out so many new behaviors, they are bound to experience some self-doubt. Although this is normal, building self-confidence enables them to lead healthy, successful lives.

Activities

● Ask the students to form pairs and take turns asking and answering the following questions: (a) Please name two things that you do well, and (b) Please describe a success in your life.

● Bring the class together. Pass out and complete the "Assess your Self-Esteem" worksheet (see Appendix G). This worksheet provides a list of statements relating to self-esteem, to which the students answer "yes" or "no."

Homework Ask the students to think of one or more things that they can do for family members to make them feel better. Ask the students to try to actually do one of the activities during the week. Ask the students to complete the "Building

Self-Esteem" worksheet (see Appendix H), which provides an outline for the student to record their experiences doing something for a family member.

INSTRUCTOR'S NOTE: This is the first session in which the students are divided into pairs. The students may feel awkward forming pairs and many will want to stay with their close friends. We suggest that students be instructed to form pairs with others that they do not know well.

Session Five: Communication Skills

Goal To build effective listening and communication skills.

Introduction to Class Review the major concepts of the previous session. Explain that the purpose of this session is to introduce students to key elements of good communicating and listening — skills that are important in order to build one's own self-confidence.

Activities

● Review some of the guidelines to good communication (maintaining eye contact, showing that you understand, asking good questions) with the class. (See Appendix I for an overview of effective communication skills.) You may wish to pass out these guidelines to students.

● Have students pair up with someone and then divide the class into two groups, with one member of each pair in each of the two groups. Privately tell one group that when they return to their partner, they are to self-disclose something of importance. Privately tell the other group that on returning to their partner, they are to deliberately violate the communication skills rules (i.e., interrupt, look away, talk to others). Allow the partners to interact in this way for several minutes.

● Bring the class together to discuss the "Partner" exercise (e.g., how it feels when someone doesn't listen to you).

Homework Have the students practice effective communication skills with family members and friends, and complete the session five "Partners" worksheet (see Appendix J). The worksheet provides an outline for the students to review the "Partner" exercise, which provides an opportunity to explore alternate ways of interacting in similar situations.

INSTRUCTOR'S NOTE: The "partner" exercise may be upsetting or disturbing to some students. For example, a particularly shy student who experiments with self-disclose only to be rebuffed by his or her partner may feel betrayed and hurt. The instructor should acknowledge feelings of hurt, provide a rationale for the exercise, and explain that every day we encounter both supportive and unsupportive listeners. Although others may not always listen effectively, we can *seek out* supportive listeners when we have something important to discuss. A thorough debriefing should provide such individuals with a better understanding of what occurred and alleviate negative feelings. In addition, the homework assignment, which encourages young people to explore alternative outcomes to the exercise, should demonstrate that skillful listening and communicating can, and often does, lead to positive interactions. If a youth appears particularly disturbed, it may be necessary to have the student repeat the exercise, either with you or the original partner, demonstrating positive communication skills (e.g., smiling, acknowledging, asking questions).

Session Six: Decision making

Goal To foster responsible decision making.

Introduction to Class Explain to the class that this session introduces decision making and the ways in which our values affect the decisions we make. Although many of our decisions are relatively small ones, they sometimes affect the rest of our lives. For example, decisions about health, grades, relationships, and using drugs can have long-term effects.

Activities

- Explain to the students that you would like them to write down at least one example of a small decision and one example of a difficult decision.
- Ask the students to share some of their small decisions (e.g., what to have for lunch) and make the point that we often make these decisions without giving them much thought because our past experiences have helped to make this process easier.
- Ask the students to share some examples of their difficult decisions (e.g., decisions about sexuality or drug use). Suggest that these decisions often require more effort because they often involve situations and concerns that we have never faced before.
- Introduce the "Stop and Think" model of decision making (see below) as a step-by-step way of dealing with such difficult decisions and situations.

The "Stop and Think" Model of Decision Making

Steps	Questions/Actions
1. *STOP:* identify the problem	What is the concern? (try to state in a positive way)
2. *THINK:* select the goal	What do I want? (brainstorm about desired solutions)
4. *CONSEQUENCE:* Think about the pros and cons	What might happen? (Look at both the positive and negative)
5. *DECISION:* Decide what to do	What is my decision? (weigh all the consequences and decide which choice is best for you)
7. *EVALUATE OUTCOME*	Did it work? (if not, try another solution)

● Explain to the class that when following these steps, it may also be helpful to talk to others in order to obtain support and relevant information, to review how they have coped with decisions in the past, and to view possible failures as feedback to begin the process again when making decisions.

● As a class, select a potentially difficult situation from the list in Appendix K (e.g., your friend wants to steal or use drugs) and use the "Stop and Think" model to make a decision regarding the situation.

INSTRUCTOR'S NOTE: At some point during this exercise, you might ask the students what advice they would give to someone who had a particularly difficult decision. This should demonstrate that there is not always a "best" choice, and that the appropriate course of action may be different from that selected by a friend. Acknowledge that in some situations, students do not have time to go through all of the steps completely, but assert that it is helpful to stop a moment and brainstorm solutions and consequences before taking any action. This makes it more likely that a good decision will be made.

Homework Have the students apply the Stop and Think model to a difficult decision that they are currently facing. Ask the students to complete the "Stop and Think" worksheet (see Appendix L), which provides an outline for them to record their actions and experiences in the decision making process.

Session Seven: Substances

Goal To provide students with information relating to mood-altering substances and the possible harmful consequences of their usage.

Introduction to Class Review the decision making skills and how they are applicable to decisions with drugs. Explain that the remaining sessions will focus on the influence of drugs on adolescents. These sessions will teach the students accurate information about drugs and describe ways in which their life skills can be applied to situations that involve substances.

Activities

● Instructors are encouraged to develop and present a discussion about drugs, and the health and social consequences of abuse as well as some of the pressures in our society to use drugs. A drug "Fact Sheet" is provided in Appendix M. (See also, Appendix A for an index of organizations and references that can provide additional drug information.)

Homework Ask the students to identify and record a pro-drug message or advertisement (e.g., for cigarettes, alcohol) in a magazine or on television. Have the students complete the "No Thanks" worksheet (see Appendix N). The worksheet asks the students to critically examine the advertisement and, based on information relating to the health hazards, generate arguments against the advertised drug.

INSTRUCTOR'S NOTE: Some youth may use the substance information and role-playing sessions as opportunities to flaunt their usage. Although this is unlikely, you may need to acknowledge that students do use some drugs. It is important that this be done in a careful, non-judgmental manner. If students perceive you as judgmental with respect to drugs, you will lose credibility with them. It will be important to provide accurate information regarding drugs and to model and reinforce nonuse.

Session Eight: Identifying the Pressures to Use Drugs

Goal To encourage students to think critically about the influence of alcohol, marijuana, cigarettes, and other drugs in our society.

Introduction to Class Review the fact sheet and answer any questions relating to substances. Explain to the students that this session will involve applying the skills reviewed in the course to situations where they feel pressure to use drugs.

Activities

● Ask the students for possible reasons why young people continue to use certain drugs, such as tobacco, even when the evidence shows that they can cause problems such as cancer or heart diseases (e.g., messages from the media, adult modeling, peer pressure).

● Review the reactions to the "No Thanks" homework assignments and ask the students what they think is the purpose of drug-related advertising. Why do some magazines (e.g., *Seventeen*) have policies that they will not advertise cigarettes, while others permit such advertisements?

● Distribute magazines to the students, asking them to locate a pro-drug advertisement. Encourage students to think about the message that is being conveyed and possible counter-arguments.

● Review other sources of influences which favor drug use (e.g., peer pressure) and discuss why friends often encourage each other to experiment with drugs.

● Ask the students to generate a list of things they could do or say that would help them resist some of the pressures to use drugs (e.g., develop counter-arguments, walk away, remind myself of my strengths, remember information about drugs, use the steps of the Stop and Think model).

Homework Encourage students to write a letter to the editor of a magazine or a television station, and let the management know if they have their support concerning depiction and advertising of drugs. (See Appendix O for examples of organizations to write to and samples of letter formats.)

INSTRUCTOR'S NOTE: Throughout the discussion of media influences and the provision of magazines, the leader should remain sensitive to the diversity of students' ethnic backgrounds. For example, depending on the racial composition of the group, it may be important to include magazines that depict Black and Hispanic models. Many publishing companies (e.g., Ebony) are willing to provide complimentary back issues to students participating in substance abuse prevention programs.

Session Nine: Resisting Peer Pressure

Goal To practice resisting peer pressures to use drugs.

Introduction to Class Review the previous section. Explain that the last session helped the class to think about the various pressures to use drugs and that in those situations the students have a choice. Today, we will explore ways to communicate openly, honestly, and directly with friends, so that we can make the choices that are best for us, express our opinions, and not jeopardize our friendships for standing up for these feelings.

Activities

● Ask the class to define peer pressure as well as the positive and negative aspects of it.

● Briefly define and list the differences between being assertive and being aggressive in peer relationships.

● Ask students to demonstrate effective peer pressure resistance situations.

Possible role-play situations

1. Some friends of yours are going to a friends' house after school to smoke some marijuana. They want you to go but you don't like smoking marijuana. What will you do and say?

2. You are with a group of friends. One of them starts passing around a pack of cigarettes. Then, someone says, "Hey, let's all light up together." You don't want to participate. What do you do and say?

3. You are watching T.V. at home with your brother. Your brother says, "Since our folks are not around, let's drink some beer?" You don't want to. What is the next thing you'd say?

(Additional examples can be found in Appendix P.)

Homework Have the students complete the "drug alternatives" worksheet (see Appendix Q), which lists reasons why people use drugs and asks students to think of one or two possible alternatives.

INSTRUCTOR'S NOTE: Throughout the role-plays, some students may indicate that they would typically *not* resist using certain drugs (e.g., cigarettes, beer). You may want to ask "What is an example of a drug that you would not want to use?" (e.g., morphine, crack). You can then suggest that he or she role play resisting that drug. Similarly, a student may say that in particular situations (e.g., at a party), he or she would *not* want to resist usage. You can ask the student, "What is an example of a situation where you would want to resist using a drug?" (e.g., before playing sports, before a final exam). You can then ask the student to apply the role play to these situations. If you have concerns about the possibility of substance abuse among such youth, it may be appropriate to administer the multiple gating scales to the students' teachers and/or parents (see chapter 4). It will be important to assure that all referral procedures be done in confidentiality so that youth do not feel singled out on the basis of their usage.

Session Ten: Overview of Course and Future Goals

Goal To review the course, and to think about future goals.

Introduction to Class Review the skills and information covered in all of the sessions, get feedback from the students, and discuss goals that the students may have for the future.

Activities

- All of the different sessions can be seen as helping youngsters improve their self-confidence and develop skills for living healthy, productive lives. Ask the students to list the most important skills that the course has helped them with.
- Ask the students to think about short- and long-term goals that they may have in their lives.
- Introduce the Goal Setting Steps as a means of working toward long- and short-term goals.

Goal Setting Steps

Goal Setting Steps	Example
Define the goal	(e.g., obtain an A in English)
Outline steps to achieve the goal	(e.g., complete all homework)
Consider the possible problems	(e.g., not enough time)
Consider ways of dealing with them	(e.g., spend less time on the telephone)
Set deadlines to achieve the goal	(e.g., end of semester)

- Ask the students to identify an admired person whom they would like to emulate in the future. Have the students think about some of the ways they could reach that long-term goal.
- Have the students form pairs, identify short-term goals that they have for the following semester, and complete the goal steps together.
- Explain that during the following session, the students will be completing posttests that will enable you to determine the influences of the Youth Skills program and areas that may need to be improved.

INSTRUCTOR'S NOTE: There are several issues that will need to be addressed during this final session, particularly if you are an outside consultant. It will be important to bring closure to the class in a way that will leave the students with a clear idea of what the class has given them and what they have contributed to the experience of the whole group. Some members may feel hurt or upset that you are leaving after they have placed trust in you. It will be important to acknowledge these feelings, and to emphasize the skills that they have learned and your appreciation of their contributions to the program. One way to facilitate a positive termination process is to give each student a certificate confirming their successful completion of the course and validating their contributions. You might want to hold a party during this session to mark the end of the course and to celebrate their acquisition of important skills. This party can be planned during session nine.

Posttesting

Goal To ascertain students' post-program levels of substance use, drug knowledge, and skills.

Activities

- Explain to the students that in order to determine the effectiveness of the program, you would appreciate their completing the surveys. Tell them that these are the same surveys that they completed at the beginning of the course, and that their answers will enable you to improve the program. Explain that their answers will remain confidential and that the information will not be used against them in any way.
- Administer the posttests.
- If your evaluation includes a control group, administer a posttest at this time. (Relevant tests for this assessment can be found in Appendix B.)

INSTRUCTOR'S NOTE: You may wish to include a retrospective pretest at this point to enhance the validity of the assessments. (See the following section for a discussion of this technique.) If you collected biochemical samples or used the bogus pipeline procedure to promote honest reporting on the pretests, it will be important to include these measures in the posttest assessment.

STAGE FOUR: EVALUATION

In the final stage, the impact of the intervention is assessed. It is unfortunate that the evaluation of applied programs is generally a low priority for many practitioners and school officials. We believe that assessment of any intervention is essential for a number of reasons. First, applied research techniques provide a method of judging the effectiveness of the intervention in reaching its goals. In addition, outcome data afford us an opportunity to make comparisons, to identify the most effective procedures, to provide a data base for further justification of preventive services, and to guide decisions about which interventions to use under what circumstances. Because we feel that program evaluation is important, the remainder of this chapter will be devoted to this topic. We will discuss the various levels of evaluation, available instruments, and some of the methodological issues associated with measuring substance use. The techniques that we are discussing are applicable to a wide range of prevention programs and evaluation goals.

Levels of Evaluation

The Prevention Branch of the National Institute on Drug Abuse (NIDA) has developed an evaluation research model that features three levels of evaluation:

process, outcome, and impact. Process evaluation includes identification of the setting and participants, a description of the services delivered, the utilization of the program, and participants' satisfaction. Process evaluation is used at points throughout the intervention to assist in the ongoing decisions to continue or modify the intervention. Often an informal procedure, such as asking students for their feelings about the program, will provide invaluable data for guiding future activities. However, sometimes a more formal, systematic data-gathering process will be required. The consumer satisfaction questionnaire, designed for students, in Figure 5.3 was designed to meet this need.

Outcome evaluation is concerned with measuring the effect of the intervention on the participants: adolescents, families, counselors, peer leaders, and teachers. Unlike process evaluation, which provides more descriptive information concerning characteristics of the actual program, outcome evaluation utilizes experimental procedures to assess the overall outcome of the intervention. The specific intent of an outcome evaluation is to show that the program has reached its original objectives. The findings of the outcome evaluation are important for those who set policy and make administrative and funding decisions that affect the future of the program.

Impact evaluation explores the aggregate effect of prevention programs on the community as a whole. The community may be defined as a school system, county, city, state, region of the country, or the nation. The purpose of impact evaluation is to assess the additive effects of the numerous substance abuse prevention programs operating within a geographic boundary, or of an individual program operating over an extended period of time. The manner in which impact data are selected is a function of the community needs and problems that gave rise to the prevention program. Broad issues such as changes in incidence and prevalence of drugs, or changes in the community's competence to deal with these problems, are frequently addressed in impact evaluation.

Initiating the Evaluation

In order to evaluate a drug abuse program, a consultant should be knowledgeable about: (a) the processes entailed in conducting the three types of evaluation, (b) the instruments available to measure process events and outcome, and (c) the wide variety of experimental designs available. We have adopted a general model (Parsons & Meyers, 1985) that depicts the processes involved in evaluating substance abuse prevention programs. It is important to note that the decisions and goals of prevention programs are most typically formed around the extent to which the program has reached its short-term objectives.

Step One: Specifying Outcomes. This step involves identifying the intervention strategies and the outcomes of the program. For example, an outcome for a school system might be: "After the students have participated in the Operation

Date_____

Name_____

1) How do you feel about the YOUTH SKILLS program?

1	2	3	4	5
very positive		*neutral*	*negative*	*very negative*

2) How would you recommend the program for other students?

1	2	3	4	5
definitely	*yes*	*not sure*	*no*	*definitely no*

3) What do you like best about the YOUTH SKILLS program?

4) What do you like least about the program?

5) Below is a list of the major topics that were covered in Youth Skills. Please check how helpful you feel that each topic was for you in resisting drug use.

	Very Helpful	Some-What	Not Very	Not At All
Adolescence	_____	_____	_____	_____
Communication	_____	_____	_____	_____
Self-Esteem	_____	_____	_____	_____
Decision Making	_____	_____	_____	_____
Resisting Pressures to use	_____	_____	_____	_____
Goal Setting	_____	_____	_____	_____

Thank you for your cooperation!

Please feel free to write any additional comments about the YOUTH SKILLS Program in the space provided below.

FIGURE 5.3. Consumer satisfaction questionnaire

Snowball program, statistically significant pre–post gains on the Assertiveness Skills Inventory will be noted."

Step Two: Selecting Instruments to Measure the Outcome. The instruments selected will depend on the intervention strategy and the desired outcomes of the program. For example, the goals of a drug education program may be to: (a) improve the students' knowledge concerning various drugs, (b) change students' drug attitudes, and (c) reduce students' levels of substance use. The goals of a community-based substance abuse prevention program may involve positively influencing the family and school environment, and enhancing students' cognitive and behavioral skills. To measure these projected outcomes, the evaluator may choose to administer a Social Climate Scale (e.g., Moos, Insel, & Humphrey, 1974) and a Life Skills Inventory (e.g., Botvin, Baker, Resnick, Filazzola, & Botvin, 1984). There are literally hundreds of standardized research instruments that may be used to collect the information needed for the process, outcome, and impact evaluations. In Appendix B, we provide an instrument that could be used to evaluate substance abuse prevention programs. The selected instrument is reliable and valid, relevant to the goals of the prevention interventions, and not difficult to administer and score.

MEASURING SUBSTANCE USAGE. Regardless of the proposed mediating variables (e.g., information, skills, school environment), the ultimate goal of most substance abuse prevention programs is to reduce and prevent substance use among adolescents. Despite the importance of this outcome, the measurement of substance use can be problematic. For example, adolescents often use drugs infrequently and episodically, and as a result it may be difficult for them to characterize their usual level of usage. They may not actually recall the number of cigarettes or drinks that they have had in recent days or weeks. Adolescents may also try to mislead the investigator and under-report substance behavior, for fear of being identified or to please the evaluator (Murray, O'Connell, Schmid, & Perry, 1987).

The adolescents' inhibitions against reporting substance use may decrease over the course of the program, confounding the comparisons of the pretests to the posttests (Rhodes & Jason, 1987). Finally, adolescents may exaggerate their levels of substance use to appear older or to be uncooperative (Murray et al., 1987). All of these factors can bias the information and render the outcome evaluations invalid.

These difficulties have prompted extensive research on methods to increase the validity of self-reports and objective measures of substance usage. In the following sections, we will review the various measurement techniques that have been developed and their applicability in applied settings.

Given the potential biases in self-reports of usage, biochemical measures are considered to be more valid and reliable than self-report indices (Cook & Campbell, 1976). For cigarette smoking, biochemical assessment methods consist of measuring the carbon monoxide in expired air and assessing the cotinine and thiocyanate in serum, urine, or saliva. Elevated carbon monoxide levels are highly related to smoking tobacco, and can be quickly and inexpensively measured using the ecolyzer. However, the carbon monoxide ions remain within a healthy individual for less than twenty-four hours, and the time is even shorter for physically active adolescents. In addition, variations in adolescent smoking patterns, as well as the influence of pollutants, marijuana, and alcohol, can produce erratic and unreliable assessments (Pechacek, Murray, Luepker, Mittlemark, Johnson, & Schutz, 1984).

Cotinine is the primary metabolite of nicotine and, when found in body fluids, is almost always related to tobacco exposure. The major problem with measuring cotinine is that it is relatively costly to analyze the samples (Haley, Axelrod, & Tilton, 1983). Thiocyanate levels in saliva are indicative of cigarettes and can be measured effectively and inexpensively in the saliva up to fourteen days after smoking. The major difficulty with using thiocyanate as a measure of smoking is the existence of many nontobacco sources, including environmental exposures to cyanide or cyanide gases, which may confound the detection of cigarette usage. In addition, cyanogen and thiocyanate are present in many foods, increasing the possibility of false positives (Pechacek et al., 1984). Overall, there is no consensus on the optimal biochemical measure of adolescent cigarette smoking, and there are practical and methodological difficulties associated with each technique.

The most widely used biochemical tests used to screen specifically for marijuana and alcohol are the Homogeneous Enzyme Immunoassay and the Spectrophotometric Test (Bittikofer & Benton, 1984). Although these techniques provide reliable information, their applicability in most settings is limited because these tests require laboratory expertise and are relatively time consuming and expensive. Furthermore, the techniques are capable of providing information only about recently ingested drugs. Finally, the Homogeneous Enzyme Immunoassay requires a urine sample and the Spectrophotometric Tests requires a blood sample from each participant. These are fairly intrusive requirements, and it is doubtful that either members of a board of education or parents would approve of such assessments.

A frequently used alternative to actual biochemical techniques is the "bogus pipeline" (Jones & Segal, 1971; Evans, Hansen, & Mittlemark, 1977). With this technique, the experimenter convinces the respondent that answers will be independently verified by a "fake" physiological measure, taken at the same time as the self-report. There are several problems associated with this technique. For example, there is a risk that rather than reporting more honestly, participants may broaden their definitions of a given behavior to include behaviors not specifically addressed on the questionnaire. Additionally, if participants discover the deception at a later measuring point, they may retaliate for this deception by intentionally distorting answers, rendering the self-report invalid. Finally, the use of deception may complicate the evaluation of primary prevention programs that depend on trust between educators and participants.

Given these difficulties with actual or "bogus" objective measures, researchers have attempted to develop the best possible self-report measures. Completely anonymous questionnaires that are responded to with no identifying information (e.g., the child's name) are often used because they are thought to lead to increased honesty and valid reporting. However, when data is collected anonymously there is no possibility of linking the pretest to the posttest and to other sources of data, such as school or police records. Another self-report technique requires the children to supply a code, such as their birthdate, on the pre- and posttests. Although this technique may compromise confidentiality, it permits the linkage of pre- and posttests. Unfortunately, researchers who have compared coded drug-usage surveys to completely anonymous surveys have found significant differences. In one study, for example, completely anonymous questionnaires resulted in higher reported levels of drug usage than did questionnaires in which there were few identifiable markings (Olson, Beaulieu, Rhodes, Nicholas, & Jason, 1986).

Another factor that appears to affect the validity of self-report measures involves possible changes in the students' willingness to report their usage. As a prevention program proceeds, there is a tendency for the participants to become more familiar and comfortable with the instructor. One consequence of this is that drug usage levels are self-reported with less inhibition on the posttest as compared to the pretest. As a result, comparisons of pre- and posttest ratings are confounded and the interpretation of the effectiveness of the intervention is compromised (Cronbach & Furby, 1970).

Rhodes and Jason (1987) were able to partially control for this bias through the utilization of the retrospective pretest in the evaluation of a substance abuse prevention program. This technique involves asking the students to answer each question on the posttest measure twice. First, they respond in reference to their current perception of themselves (post). Immediately after responding in this manner, the students answer the same questions again, this time in reference to how they perceive themselves to have been just before the intervention began (retrospective pretest) (Howard, Schmeck, & Bray, 1979). These tests are administered close to each other in time, increasing the likelihood that both ratings are made from the same perspective, with the same level of inhibition and honesty.

Overall, there are many potential biases that could influence self-reported drug use. The inhibitions of some students may decrease over the course of the program, while others may feel that there are too many risks associated with reporting illegal or socially condemned behaviors. Although self-reports are simple, efficient and inexpensive, these biases often render them invalid. Evaluators can reduce the biases by using anonymous or coded instruments and by assuring the students that their responses are confidential and will not be used against them. The retrospective pretest and biochemical measures can also control for some biases, and, when used in conjunction with the traditional self-report measures, can provide the researcher with a comprehensive picture of the program's impact.

INTENSITY OF ASSESSMENT. We have reviewed a wide range of techniques and instruments that can be used to assess the impact of a substance abuse prevention program. An evaluation could potentially range from simply asking students to discuss the effects of the program to a comprehensive evaluation that includes traditional self-reports, role-played assessments of skills (Hops, Weissman, Biglan, Faller, & Severson, 1986), a retrospective pretest, and biochemical measures. See Figure 5.4.

The consultant's decision concerning the intensity of the assessment frequently depends on: (a) the goals of intervention (e.g., increasing knowledge, modifying skills, and/or influence on the ecological context); (b) the intended use of the findings (e.g., scientific journals, agency accountability); (c) the resources of the consultant (e.g., knowledge of statistical design, available time), and the overall constraints of the setting (e.g., budgetary limitations, policies concerning consent or biochemical assessment). The level of assessment ultimately determines the confidence with which the consultant can draw conclusions about the findings and generalize these findings to other settings.

Step Three: Identifying an Appropriate Design. In order to properly interpret the findings from a drug prevention study, an appropriate evaluation design needs to be employed. Although research designs with large samples and randomized assignment of children, classrooms, or schools to different conditions can give the evaluator considerable control over threats to internal and external validity — and thus allow for certainty and generality of program effectiveness — most evaluators must work within considerable constraints. The quasi-experimental approaches presented by Campbell and Stanley (1966) offer a useful compromise between the evaluator's need for a carefully controlled, experimental design and the program staff's need for flexibility.

For readers interested in more information on this topic, the Prevention Evaluations Guidelines (French et al., 1979) provide a thorough discussion of the objectives, design, instruments, and methodology involved in evaluating substance abuse prevention programs. In addition, Hall, Hawkins, and Axelrod (1975) offer a time-series design approach particularly applicable to the evaluation of school and agency-based programs. Finally, Cohen and Cohen (1983) provide useful evaluation guidelines.

Step Four: Decision making and Dissemination. Once the data have been collected and appropriate analyses performed, the findings need to be interpreted. At this stage, the evaluator needs to assess the validity of the evaluation and potential weaknesses in the data collection procedures or the design. Based on

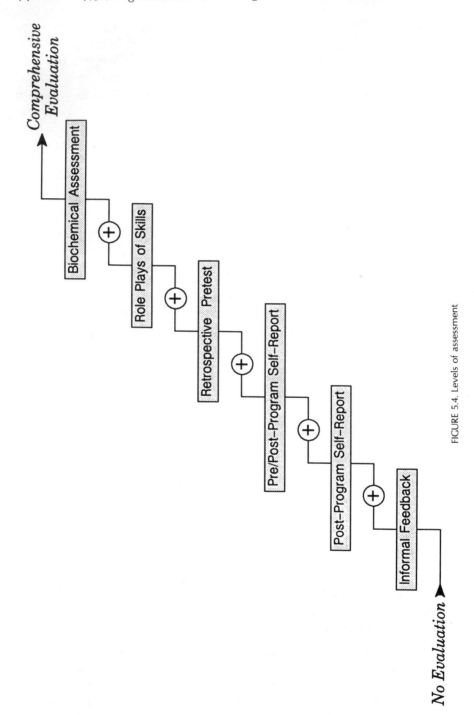

FIGURE 5.4. Levels of assessment

the findings, the evaluator can identify the outcomes achieved and make decisions about the specific changes that could be made in the program. In addition to using the findings for continued program development, the consultant should always provide written and verbal feedback to all agency staff involved with the program. This feedback may, in turn, provide the basis for continued program implementation.

Chapter 6

Future Directions

Throughout this book, we have noted that drug use occurs not in isolation, but within the context of developmental, community, school, family, and peer influences. Within this framework, we provided a social stress model of substance abuse that can help readers identify and predict those factors affecting substance usage among youth. According to this model, adolescents initiate substance use as a means of coping with a variety of stressors, which may arise from within the family, the school, the peer group, or the community. Adolescents are less likely to engage in problematic early usage as a means of coping with these stressors if: (a) they have made positive attachments with their families, teachers, and peers; (b) they have the skills to cope with the stressors; and (c) they have sufficient resources, opportunities, and successful role models in their communities. Alternately, if the process of developing positive attachments has been interrupted, impeded, or damaged by uncaring or inconsistent parents or teachers; if external stressors exceed the youngsters' ability to cope with them effectively; or if the school and community offer few resources and models for success, adolescents may have less confidence in their ability to cope with stressors, and be more likely to use drugs.

The social stress model can help us understand the etiology and maintenance of substance abuse among children and adolescents. In addition, this general model can be extended to other problem behaviors (e.g., drop-out, delinquency), all of which can be viewed as ineffective strategies for coping with the stressors of adolescence.

This model also provides us with a framework for assessing interventions that seek to prevent drug abuse among adolescents. Preventive strategies have been implemented at several levels, many of which were reviewed in chapter 3. Most interventions have attempted to enhance social coping skills, whereas others have focused on facilitating more positive attachment to the families and the school system. In our review, we suggested that comprehensive strategies with an impact on all levels of the problem, offer the most promise for preventing substance abuse among adolescents.

FUTURE TRENDS IN DRUG ABUSE

Our model can also be used to help predict social trends in adolescent substance abuse. Noticing and predicting such trends might enable us to better plan the types of substance abuse prevention programs that will be needed in the upcoming years. Before predicting future trends in substance abuse, it is important to note that societies often experience cyclical patterns of substance use. For example, from 1885 to 1920 the United States experienced an epidemic of narcotics and cocaine use, and another epidemic of use occurred in the mid-1960s. More than twenty years later, we may be seeing a shift in this trend (Musto, 1987).

Outside of the poorest neighborhoods, the widespread use of illegal drugs among our nation's youth is declining. Marijuana use peaked in 1978, and by 1985 7 out of 10 high school seniors believed marijuana use to be harmful. In addition, use of hallucinogens, like LSD and PCP, has fallen since 1979.

In a national survey, 15-to-25 year olds were asked if they had smoked marijuana in the last month (Voss, 1985). Those who were better educated were less likely to say that they were using marijuana. Among an earlier generation, who probably developed their attitudes toward marijuana in the late 1960s and early 1970s, the findings were just the reverse. Johnston, O'Malley, and Bachman (1986) asked high school seniors whether they had used drugs other than marijuana in the previous month. They found that seniors in 1986 were using drugs less than seniors in 1981. The greatest change had taken place among those youth whose parents had some graduate education (i.e., drug use decreased from 36.7% to 23.7%). The least change took place among students whose parents had never been to high school (i.e. decreases from 25.4% to 22.7%). (See Figure 6.1).

These findings indicate a new trend, which carries a message of hope for the more educated and affluent. Relatively privileged American youth are beginning to turn away from the use of illegal drugs. At the same time, lower SES and minority youth are experiencing fewer changes in drug use patterns. If this trend continues, the drug issue may become less visible to many Americans, and thus receive less attention from government. As with the use of crack in recent years, it is often the threat to middle- and upper-middle-class adolescents that elevates issues to the public agenda. In the coming years, mental health practitioners will need to maintain their vigilance concerning problems of substance abuse among low SES and minority youth, particularly if the problem decreases among the middle class and thus captures less attention from public policy officials and funding agencies.

Preventing Substance Abuse among Low SES and Minority Youth

Many researchers have argued that prevention efforts should be better tailored to the served populations (Bobo, 1986; NIAAA, 1981). Unfortunately, virtually all of the substance abuse prevention research has been conducted with predominately White, middle-class populations (Botvin & Wills, 1985). Future efforts will need to be focused on developing and evaluating programs that are applicable to low SES and minority populations, many of whom are more at risk for becoming substance abusers. Practitioners who fail to acknowledge basic social realities confronting the poor and minorities may find it difficult to gain credibility with these youth.

Substance abuse prevention programs for low SES and minority youth need to be designed in ways that avoid value conflicts. For example, assertiveness is commonly emphasized during communication skills training. Yet, in some cultures, children are taught that in many situations such behavior is disrespectful. Bobo (1986) provides a framework for designing and implementing culturally-sensitive substance abuse prevention programs.

Concluding Remarks

Substance abuse among youth is a complex, multidimensional phenomenon that presents a significant challenge to mental health, legal, and social systems in

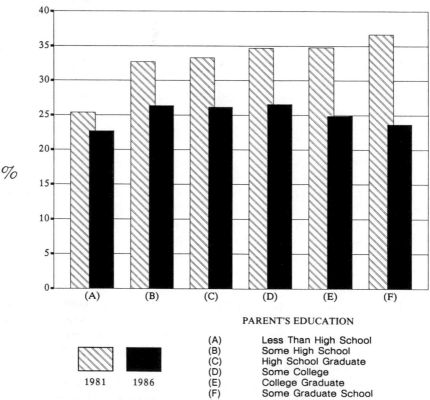

FIGURE 6.1. Trends in substance abuse. Data from: Johnston, L. D., O'Malley, P. M., & Bachman, J. G. (1986). *Drug use among American high school students, college students, and other young adults: National trends through 1985.* Rockville, MD: National Institute on Drug Abuse, DHEW # (ADM) 86–1450.

contemporary society. Meeting this challenge will involve incorporating our current knowledge concerning the development of adolescent substance abuse with comprehensive primary prevention strategies. The first step in this process is a recognition that substance use occurs, not in isolation, but within the context of developmental, family, school, peer, and community influences. With this recognition, it becomes clear that our most effective strategies for preventing substance abuse are those that focus not only on the youth but on the ecological contexts of which they are a part. As Konopka (1981) stated:

> When we recognize the multiple causation of problems and realize that the causes lie neither exclusively in the individual nor in the social structure, it becomes clear that a profession which works toward social justice in a wide sense must feel responsibility for amelioration and social changes (p. 195).

This will require that practitioners develop and implement comprehensive substance abuse prevention programs that address not only the youth and community variables but the social policies and institutions that impinge on these variables. Considerable progress has been made with respect to substance abuse prevention programs. Early experiences in prevention demonstrated that teaching students about the dangers of drugs had virtually no effect on substance usage. In recent years, more successful skills-based prevention programs have been developed that provide youth with the competencies and skills necessary to critique peer norms and make thoughtful decisions about their health, relationships, and future goals. Such programs recognize youngsters' developmental needs and thus provide skills and opportunities for growth-enhancing limit testing.

Community-based programs seek to incorporate skills-training strategies into comprehensive, ecological programs. These programs blend the knowledge of the mental health professional with the strengths and needs of the participants. Participants are encouraged to become active owners of both the process and the content of the program (Kelly, 1987). By working with the school and community participants at all stages of the prevention process, the programs attempt to influence not only the youth but the norms and contingencies of the surrounding community. Participants become advocates for change, resources remain within the community, and behaviors and skills are more likely to be maintained beyond the classroom setting. Given these potential benefits, we view community-based programs as a promising step in the prevention of substance abuse among youth.

Despite these advances, prevention programs rarely address some of the basic social and institutional factors that impede youthful adjustment. For example, inferior education in our country, particularly in the inner cities, produces thousands of inadequately prepared youngsters who have difficulties competing for the types of jobs that could raise their economic status. These youth must cope not only with unemployment but with pervasive pressure to engage in problem behaviors such as drug abuse, unprotected sexuality, and excessive risk taking. Similarly, many youth are forced to live in slum neighborhoods, where they are influenced by multi-problem families, poor coping models, high levels of unemployment, and few opportunities. This suggests that one target for our comprehensive prevention efforts might be some of the social and economic barriers that confront many of our youth within inner-city areas. As professionals, we have information that could be used to convince executive and legislative decision makers to alter some of the deleterious influences on youth (Konopka, 1981). For example, research findings concerning the factors causing excessively high school dropout rates can be used to influence educational policies and budgetary decisions (Sween, Kyle, & Reyes, 1987).

A sensitivity to the concerns of youth and a commitment to comprehensive prevention efforts will enable us to stroll past elementary school playgrounds with a sense of hope and confidence. We can hope that the children will have teachers that encourage their growing sense of wonder and are responsive to their needs and fears. We can hope that at the end of the day, the children will be going to homes and neighborhoods that are rich in opportunities and rewards; and that within these contexts the children will acquire a broad repertoire of skills that they can draw on to cope with the stressors that they will encounter. We can hope that young people will develop a positive network of support from which they can actively pursue healthy challenges and risks throughout adolescence and adulthood. Finally, we can feel confident that, in promoting healthy behavior and preventing obstacles to adjustment, we will be working toward a better future for these and other young people.

Appendixes

Appendix A:
Additional Resources

ORGANIZATIONS

Alcohol and Drug Abuse Education Program, U.S. Department of Education. The "School Team" approach offered in this program is designed to increase local schools' capability to present and reduce drug and alcohol abuse and associated disruptive behaviors. Five regional centers provide training and technical assistance to local school districts.

U.S. Department of Education
Alcohol and Drug Abuse Education Program
400 Maryland Avenue, SW
Washington, DC 20202-4101

American Council on Drug Education (ACDE) organizes conferences, develops media campaigns; publishes books, a quarterly newsletter, and education kits for physicians, schools, and libraries.

5820 Hubbard Drive
Rockville, MD 20852

Center for Community Change links community groups with community development techniques. The center concentrates on the problems facing low-income communities, and provides training in prevention strategies and advocacy.

100 Wisconsin Ave, NW
Washington, DC 20007

Center for Multi-Cultural Awareness (CMA) (project of National Institute on Drug Abuse). Identifies, develops, and adopts culturally relevant materials for drug abuse prevention, provides technical assistance to agencies and to local programs serving minorities; training offered in networking and coalition building.

U.S. Department of Education
Black Concerns Staff
Hubert Humphrey Building
200 Independence Ave., SW
Washington, DC 20201

Committees of Correspondence, Inc. provides a newsletter that contains substance abuse research updates, ideas, and contacts.

57 Conant Street, Room 113
Danvers, MA 09123

Families In Action maintains a drug information center and publishes *Drug Abuse Update,* a newsletter containing abstracts of articles published in medical and academic journals.

3845 North Druid Hills Road, Suite 300
Decatur, GA 30033

National Clearinghouse For Drug Abuse Information. Resource center for collecting and distributing substance abuse materials. Services include computer searches and special interest packages.

P.O. Box 1706
Rockville, MD 20850

National Federation of Parents For Drug-Free Youth (NFP), an umbrella parent organization, publishes and distributes the Parent Group Starter Kit, a newsletter, lists of parent groups, and brochures on substances.

P.O. Box 722
Silver Spring, MD 20901

National Institute On Drug Abuse (NIDA) conducts surveys on drug abuse; publishes numerous education and informational materials; supports research on substance abuse.

U.S. Department of Health and Human Services (HHS)
National Institute on Drug Abuse (NIDA)
5600 Fishers Lane
Rockville, MD 20857

National Self-Help Resource Center provides community groups and organizations with information and bibliographies on networking, program development, and community organization.

200 S. ST., NW
Washington, DC 20009

Parents Resource Institute For Drug Education (PRIDE), a very active parent group, publishes a newsletter with a national overview and produces and distributes course materials.

Robert W. Woodroff Building, Room 1216

100 Edgewood Avenue

Atlanta, GA 30303

Pyramid Project (funded by NIDA) provides assistance and information on the following topics: community management and staff development, technical assistance for substance abuse prevention programs, media campaigns, needs assessment and community organization, research and evaluation strategies, prevention curricula, funding resources, and training.

7101 Wisconsin Ave.

Suite 1006

Bethesda, MD. 20014

PUBLICATIONS RELEVANT TO
DEVELOPING PREVENTION CURRICULA

Hawley, R. A. (1984). *A school answers back: Responding to student drug use.* Rockville, MD: Government Printing Office.

Curricula guidelines for teachers, counselors, consultants, administrators, and parents; $7.95, available from the American Council for Drug Education, 6193 Executive Boulevard, Rockville, MD 20852.

Scott, S. (1985). *Peer pressure reversal.* Human resource Center: Amherst, MA.

Provides instruction on teaching refusal skills to children and adolescents; $9.95, available through publisher.

Manatt, M. (1983). *Parents, peers, and pot II: Parent in action.* Rockville, MD: Government Printing Office.

Describes strategies for forming parent and community groups in rural, suburban, and urban settings; $1, available through PRIDE.

U.S. Department of Education (1986). *What works: Schools without drugs.* Washington DC: Government Printing Office.

Provides an overview of the problem and recommendations for preventing substance use in the schools; Free, available through Schools Without Drugs, Pueblo, CO, 81009.

COMPREHENSIVE SKILLS-BASED
CURRICULA

Quest International

Quest International markets two prevention programs, *Skills for Adolescence* (for students in grades 6–8) and *Skills for Living* (for high school students). *Skills for Adolescence* offers positive growth experiences and teaches specific coping skills, with a special emphasis on preventing substance abuse. The course focuses on seven units (each composed of approximately 8 sessions) including: (a) entering the teen years, (b) building self-confidence, (c) learning about emotions, (d) improving peer relationships, (e) strengthening family relationships, (f) developing critical thinking skills, and (g) setting goals for healthy living. In addition, the program places a strong emphasis on the development of school and community projects in which students offer service to others. The program provides a detailed training manual, a student textbook and workbook, parent seminars, and technical assistance.

Skills for Living focuses on helping high school students acquire four major competencies: a) self-discipline, b) responsibility, c) good judgment, and d) the ability to interact effectively with others. The curriculum covers basic skills for effective living, concentrating on:

1. Building self-concept
2. Dealing with emotions
3. Building constructive relationships
4. Preparing for family life
5. Building trust and commitment
6. Successful parenting
7. Understanding financial management
8. Goal setting and life planning
9. Developing a personal perspective.

In addition, the program provides teacher training, opportunities for parent involvement, community service, and intensive student leadership training.

Additional information concerning these programs is available through THE QUEST NATIONAL CENTER, 6655 Sharon Woods, Blvd., Columbus, OH 43229-7019.

Project Star (Students Taught Awareness And Resistance)

Project Star is an experimental research and demonstration project developed by the University of Southern California's Health Behavior Research Institute. (See section on Pentz et. al in chapter 3 for a discussion of the theoretical rationale, specific techniques, and evaluation of this approach.) The focus of the project is on the prevention of drug abuse among youth by teaching students how to deal with and resist different forms of peer pressure in a variety of situations. Students first learn key concepts and practice identifying pressure situations. They then observe role models demonstrating simple techniques for resisting pressure. Finally, students practice the resistance skills and apply them to a variety of situations. The program is implemented by peer leaders, who are identified by students and provided leadership training. The curriculum contains 10 lessons:

1. Introduction
2. Consequences of drug use and non-use

3. The facts about drugs
4. Techniques — how to say "no"
5. Peer pressure resistance
6. Changing norms to non-use
7. Advertising influences
8. Developing anti-drug commercials
9. Identifying adult influences
10. Videotaping of students resisting drug offers.

The program includes a student manual and workbook, a parent workbook, student/parent workbooks, community outreach projects, and technical assistance. Additional information is available through Marion Laboratories, Inc., P.O. Box 8480, Kansas City, MI, 64114.

Life Skills Training, (LST)

This is an experimental research and demonstration program, developed at the Cornell University Medical College. The program seeks to facilitate the development of generic life skills as well as skills and knowledge more specifically related to substance use. (See section on Botvin in chapter 3 for a discussion of the theoretical rationale, specific techniques, and evaluation of this program.) The LST program incorporates a curriculum to teach a wide range of personal and social skills, in order to improve youth's general competence and reduce potential motivations for substance use. Specific applications of these skills are practiced in social pressure situations. The general cognitive–behavioral skills incorporated into the LST Program include techniques for (a) enhancing self-esteem (e.g., goal setting, behavioral change techniques, increasing positive self-statements); (b) resisting persuasive appeals (e.g., identifying persuasive appeals, formulating counter-arguments); (c) coping with anxiety (e.g., relaxation training, mental rehearsal); (d) verbal and nonverbal communication skills; and (e) a variety of other social skills (e.g. initiating social interactions, communication skills, complimenting, assertiveness skills). These skills are taught using a combination of instruction, modeling, and rehearsal. The LST program also teaches students skills and knowledge more specifically related to the problem of substance abuse. For example, in addition to teaching students general assertive skills, students are taught how to use these skills to resist direct interpersonal pressure to use drugs. The program includes a training manual, student workbooks, and extensive technical assistance. Additional information is available through Smithfield Press, P.O. Box 211, New York, New York, 10065.

Here's Looking at You, 2000

Here's Looking at You, 2000 is a comprehensive prevention program that contains curricula and training guidelines for implementing curricula in grades K–12. The program is based on the theoretical assumption that early positive attachments to parents and teachers and skill enhancement can offset the pressures to use drugs throughout childhood and adolescence. The kindergarten-through-elementary-school components of the program emphasize early bonding with parents, through parent training and parent involvement in the classroom prevention activities. The high school component emphasizes training in specific life skills, including (a) enhancing self-esteem, (b) coping strategies, (c) decisionmaking, (d) identifying pressures to use drugs, (e) effective communication, (f) peer-pressure resistance, and (g) goal setting. The program includes a comprehensive training curricula, videos, workbooks, and technical assistance. Additional information is available through HERE'S LOOKING AT YOU, 366 Paul Avenue, Seattle, Washington 07401.

FILMS AND VIDEOTAPES

(Check with libraries for films and videos that may be available locally.)

Breaking free. For grades seven through twelve; 22 minutes; includes information brochure; $195; available through PRIDE (see organizations).

Epidemic: Kids, drugs, and alcohol. For youth and adults; 27 minutes; 16mm. $495; video $450; 3 day loan $25; available through PRIDE.

Epidemic: America fights back. Fighting drug use in the community, the workplace, and the schools; 51 minutes; 16mm. $750; video $675; 3 day loan $25; available through PRIDE. Two other segments available on community action and business and industry programs.

Wasted: A true story. For elementary through middle school grades; 22 minutes; available through the American Council for Drug Education.

How to talk to your kids about growing up without drugs and alcohol. Offers approaches to improving family communication, particularly with respect to adolescent drug and alcohol use; video $25; available through the National Federation of Parents for Drug Free Youth (NFP).

TOLL-FREE INFORMATION

1-800-554-KIDS (The National Federation of Parents for Drug-Free Youth (NFP) information line). A national information and referral service; focuses on preventing substance abuse among adolescence as well as assistance to anyone concerned about a child already using substances.

1-800-241-9746 (The Parent's Resource Institute for Drug Education [PRIDE] information line). Refers concerned parents to parent groups in their local area, gives information on how parents can form a group in their community, provides telephone consulting and referrals, and maintains a series of drug information messages which callers can listen to, free of charge.

1-800-638-2045 (The National Institute on Drug Abuse (NIDA) information line). Provides technical assistance to individuals and groups wishing to start prevention programs. Currently, the program focuses on the establishment of "Just Say No to Drugs" clubs.

1-800-662-HELP (NIDA Hotline) provides confidential information and referrals, directs callers to treatment centers in the local community, and provides free material on drug abuse.

1-800-COCAINE (Cocaine Helpline) provides referral services, guidance, and information concerning cocaine addiction.

FUNDING RESOURCES

Obtaining initial and ongoing funding for substance abuse prevention programs usually requires exploring many sources. We recommend that you seek funds from a variety of public and private, local, state, and federal sources, rather than relying on any one source. The following selected list of funding sources, agencies is brief but can provide a beginning point for your fundseeking efforts.

Public

Federal agencies make direct project awards to community applicants. State and county agencies are also recipients of federal funds, as well as of income generated from State and local taxes.

Federal

> U.S. Department of Agriculture
> Division of Agricultural Economics and Rural Sociology
> Community Affairs Extension
> 204 Weaver Building
> Pennsylvania State University
> University Park, PA 16801

The Federal Assistance Program Retrieval System (FAPRS) is a computerized system that provides a means of identifying Federal programs that could be used to meet a community's developmental needs. It researches and organizes current Federal funding data by specific program and specific state rather than giving information on all the Federal programs and funding sources that are available.

> U.S. Department of Justice
> Law Enforcement Assistance Administration (LEAA)
> Office of Juvenile Justice and Delinquency
> Prevention (OJJDP)
> 633 Indiana Ave., NW
> Washington, DC. 20005

LEAA funds projects that deal directly with juvenile delinquency prevention. LEAA has worked in partnership with the states and localities by providing three main categories of funding: planning funds, block grant funds, and discretionary funds. The major categories cover comprehensive planning, juvenile crime prevention programs, and innovative projects that supplement state comprehensive plans.

U.S. Department of Transportation (DOT)
National Highway Traffic Safety Administration
400 7th St. SW
Washington, DC 20590

DOT provides funding for prevention programs, and disseminates information, related to substance use and driving. High rates of traffic injuries and fatalities among youth are particular concern to the Department.

U.S. Department of Health and Human Services (HHS)
National Institute on Drug Abuse (NIDA)
5600 Fishers Lane
Rockville, MD 20857

Part of the Alcohol, Drug Abuse, and Mental Health Administration (ADAMHA) of the Public Health Service, U.S. Department of Health and Human Services (HHS). The various offices and services within this Department provide the primary federal funding sources for drug abuse prevention research, activities, and demonstration programs.

U.S. Department of Education
200 Independence Ave., S.W.
Washington, DC 20201

Provides funding for demonstration projects that deal directly with preventing substance abuse in the school systems, including planning funds, block grant funds, and discretionary funds.

State. At the state level, the Department of Alcoholism and Substance Abuse (DASA), the State Alcoholism Authority (SAA), or Single State Agency (SSA) award funding to local projects. These offices may be willing to finance specific projects that propose innovative approaches in the prevention of substance abuse. An additional resource is the state Department of Education. An education program coordinator in that department may be able to suggest resources available for local programs. The state Department of Social Health Services, which disburses state liquor and tobacco tax revenues, also provides prevention funds. Legislation in some States mandates that a certain percentage of these revenues be applied to substance abuse prevention activities.

County. County substance abuse agencies often receive state funds. Similarly, mental health agencies receive state funding that may be available for substance abuse prevention activities.

Private Funds

Along with state and local governments, community service organizations, businesses, and commercial companies have recognized substance abuse among youth as a serious problem. They are likely to express their concerns by allocating funds for local prevention projects. Although these private sources will vary across the country, we can suggest some national foundations and organizational sources.

National Associations
American Teachers Association
National Education Association (NEA)
1201 16th St. NW
Washington, DC 20036

National Bankers Association
900 L'Enfant Plaza, Suite 1120
Washington, DC 20024

National Business League
4324 Georgia Ave, NW
Washington, DC 20011

National Insurance Association
2400 Michigan Ave
Chicago, Ill 60616

National Medical Association
2109 E. St., NW
Washington, DC 20037

National Newspaper Publishers Association
770 National Press Building
Washington, DC 20004

Foundations. Selected private foundations support preventive efforts. An example of such support is the Smithers Foundations in New York that is dedicated to substance-related issues. Quite often, foundations specify one or more target population that they plan to support. Examine their priorities and carefully determine if your proposed program fits within their objectives.

Other Private Sources. Program planners may wish to consider the following other sources:

United Way
1343 H St. NW
Washington, DC 20005
This agency has a regular and emergency grant program and assists community organizations in obtaining funds to sustain their programs.

Foundations Center
1001 Connecticut Ave, NW
Washington DC 20036

This group specializes in assisting minority programs and prevention efforts in the inner city. It is particularly helpful in locating grant and funding sources.

McDonald's Restaurants
Corporate Contributions Division
McDonald's Plaza
Oak Brook, Ill 60521

McDonald's National Contributions Program helps local groups identify, develop, implement, and disseminate new approaches and programs that address social problems.

State and Local Groups. Support for projects may come from organizations or corporations that have incorporated substance abuse prevention into their goals and objectives. Costs for specific project needs, such as print material, might be shared with several community organizations. Funds and other assistance may be available through a variety of commercial sources such as local breweries and related businesses.

PUBLICATIONS RELEVANT TO
GRANT DEVELOPMENT

Federal domestic assistance catalogue. (1986). Washington DC: U.S. Government Printing Office.

The foundation directory. (1975). Available through The Foundation Center, 888 Seventh Ave., New York City, N.Y. 10019.

Grant Programs. Available through the National Clearinghouse for Drug Abuse Information.

Flanagan, J. (1980). *The grassroots fundraising book.* Baltimore, MD: NTWA Publications.

A guide to fundraising and proposal writing. Available through the Independent Consultants, P.O. Box 1414, Hampton, Ark. 71744.

Handbook on fund raising. Available through the National Council on Alcoholism, 733 Third Ave., New York, NY 10017.

How to get money for arts and humanities, drug and alcohol abuse and health. Available through the Human Resources Network, Chilton Book Co., 2010 Chancellor St., Philadelphia PA 19103.

Appendix B:
Evaluation Measures

STUDENT QUESTIONNAIRE

The Life Skills Training Student Questionnaire (Botvin et al., 1984) is recommended for researchers interested in obtaining a comprehensive assessment of students' skills, as well as relevant substance related information. The measure was developed for use on a research project funded by the National Institute on Drug Abuse, grant # DA02835.

This inventory contains scales designed to assess students' substance usage, substance knowledge, and attitudes about substances. In addition, the inventory contains several different scales designed to assess a number of cognitive variables which have been linked with adolescent substance use (Botvin, 1985a). Assertiveness is measured using a shortened (20-item) version of the Assertion Inventory (Gambrill & Richey, 1975). Locus of control is measured by means of a 24-item Norwicki–Strickland Locus of Control Scale for Children (1973). Social Anxiety is measured by means of seven situation-specific items relating to social situations which might produce anxiety. Self-esteem is measured using self-ratings in response to 10 descriptive statements (e.g., smart, popular, good looking) (Wells & Marwell, 1976). Self-confidence and self-satisfaction are measured using three descriptive statements (e.g., "I am able to handle difficult situations"). Substance use influenceability is measured using three items concerning the respondents' propensity to give in to social pressure. General influenceability is measured using five items relating to the extent to which the respondent is influenced by others to make an important decision. With the exception of locus of control, all of the personality variables are measured using 5-point Likert-type scales. All of these items have been used in previous research and have test-retest reliabilities ranging from .66 to .78 (Botvin et al., 1984). Depending on the program content and goals, the complete questionnaire, or sections of it, can be administered.

The scoring procedures for most of the sections are self explanatory, and evaluators should be able to determine directions of improvement if the measure is administered on a pre- to post-test basis.

STUDENT QUESTIONNAIRE SCORING GUIDELINES

The scoring procedures of each section are set up so that the higher the score, the higher the overall risk for substance abuse.

Parts I and II—These sections provide a general measure of cigarette and alcohol usage and serve as an index of changes in levels and frequency of usage.

Part I

—Items 1, 2, 4, and 6 should be inverted such that a response of 1 is 2 and 2 is scored as 1. On item 10, a response of 1 is scored as 3 and a response of 3 is scored as 1.

—On item 3, an overall score of 30 or above should be scored as 2, and 29 or below should be scored as 1.

—On item 5, an overall score of 7 or above should be scored as 2, and 6 or below should be scored as 1.

—On item 7, a score of 2 should be given to responses of 1 or more, and a response of 1 should be scored as 2.

—On item 8, the score should correspond with the response circled, but a response of 5 should be scored as 1.

—On items 9 and 10, the score should correspond with the response circled.

Part II

—Items 1, 2, 3, 4, 9, and 11 should be inverted.

—On items 5, 6, 8, and 10, the score should correspond with the response circled.

—On item 7, a response of 1 or 2 should be scored as 2, a response of 3 and 4 should be scored as 3, and a response of 5 should be assigned as 1.

Part III—This is a measure of drug knowledge. A high score indicates limited knowledge about substances and presumably an increased likelihood of usage. The answers are as follows: (1) F, (2) T, (3) T, (4) T, (6) F, (7) F, (8) T, (9) T, (10) T, (11) F, (12) F, (13) T, (14) T, (15) T, (16) T, (17) T, (18) F, (19) F, (20) F. Correct responses should be scored as 1 and incorrect responses as 2.

Part IV—This is a measure of assertiveness, a known correlate of substance usage. A high score indicates low levels of assertiveness and presumably a high likelihood of usage.

Each of the responses on this section should be inverted, such that a response of 1 is scored as 5, 2 as 4, 4 as 2, and 5 as 1.

Part V—These scales measure the individual's attitudes toward drugs. A high score indicates positive attitudes and presumably an increased likelihood of usage. The values should remain the same as the number circled, with the exception of items 1, 2, 9, 10, 11, 16, 19, and 22, whose values should be inverted.

Part VI—This is a measure of self-esteem, a known correlate of substance usage. A high score indicates a low level of self-esteem and presumably an increased likelihood of usage. All of the responses on this section should be inverted, with the exception of items 7, 9, 10, 13, 14, 15, 16, and 19, whose values should remain the same as the number circled.

Part VII—This is a measure of marijuana usage and serves as an index of changes in levels and frequency of usage. The values assigned to items 1, 2, 3, 4, and 7 should be inverted. The values assigned to items 5 and 6 should remain the same as the number circled.

Part VIII—This is a measure of drug knowledge. A high score indicates limited knowledge about drugs and presumably an increased likelihood of usage. The answers are as follows: (1) T, (2) F, (3) F, (4) T, (5) F, (6) T, (7) F, (8) F, (9) T, (10) F. Correct responses should be scored as 1 and incorrect responses as 2.

Part IX—This is a measure of locus of control, a known correlate of substance usage. A high score indicates that the individual does not possess a strong sense of inner control, and presumably is at increased risk for substance usage. The following responses should be scored as 1: (1) yes, (2) no, (3) no, (4) yes, (5) yes, (6) no, (7) no, (8) no, (9) no, (10) yes, (11) no, (12) no, (13) no, (14) no, (15) yes, (16) no, (17) yes, (18) no, (19) no, (20) yes, (21) no, (22) yes, (23) no, (24) yes. The remainder should be scored as 2.

Part X—This is a measure of attitudes towards drugs. A high score indicates positive attitudes and presumably an increased likelihood of usage. Answers to items 7, 8, and 10 should be inverted, and the remainder should be assigned the same value as the number circled.

Part XI—This is a measure of socioeconomic status. This factor can interact with other risk factors to exacerbate their influence.
—On item 1, a response of 1 should be scored as 1, a response of 2 or 3 should be scored as 2, and a response of 4 should be scored as 3.
—On items 2 and 3, a response of 1 should be scored as 3, a response of 2 should be scored as 2, a response of 3 should be scored as 1, and a response of 4 should be scored as 0.
—On items 4 and 5, the scores of the responses should be inverted.
—On item 6, a response of 2 should be scored as 1, all other response should be scored as 2.
—On items 7 and 8, a response of 5 should be scored as 1, and the remainder should be assigned the same value as the number circled.
—On items 9–16, responses should be assigned the value of the number circled, with the exception of items 9, 12, and 16, in which a response of 5 should be scored as 0 and item 13, in which a response of 4 should be scored as 0

LIFE SKILLS TRAINING
STUDENT QUESTIONNAIRE

This is not a test. DO NOT PUT YOUR NAME ON
THIS SURVEY. The code number we will give you to
stick on the top of this page will allow us to keep
your name *secret*. We want to know what you
really think, so please answer all the questions
honestly.

1. I am a: (1) boy   (2) girl   (8)

2. Write the name of your school

   here:_____

3. Teacher's Name:_____   (9)

4. Period#:_____

5. Today's Date:_____

PART I

Please answer the following questions. *Circle your answer.* Remember,
everything you say is *SECRET*. Nobody will find out what you say.

1. Have you ever smoked a cigarette?
   (1) Yes   (2) No   (10)

2. Did you smoke any cigarettes in the last month?
   (1) Yes   (2) No   (11)

3. If yes, how many did you smoke?_____ (12–14)

4. Did you smoke any cigarettes in the last week?
   (1) Yes   (2) No   (15)

5. If yes, how many did you smoke?_____ (16–18)

6. Did you smoke any cigarettes yesterday?
   (1) Yes   (2) No   (19)

7. If yes, how many did you smoke?_____ (20–21)

8. How often do you generally smoke?   (22)
   (1) Never
   (2) A few a month
   (3) A few a week
   (4) Every day
   (5) Used to but quit

9. How many of your friends smoke cigarettes?   (23)
   (1) None
   (2) A few
   (3) Some
   (4) Most
   (5) All

10. How would your parents feel if they found out you smoked cigarettes? (24)
    (1) Not mad at all
    (2) Sort of mad
    (3) Really mad

PART II

Please answer the following questions about drinking alcohol (beer, wine, hard liquor). Whatever you say will be kept private.

1. Have you ever had a drink of alcohol?
   (1) Yes   (2) No   (25)

2. Have you had a drink of alcohol in the last year?
   (1) Yes   (2) No   (26)

3. Have you had a drink of alcohol in the last month?
   (1) Yes   (2) No   (27)

4. Have you had a drink of alcohol in the last week?
   (1) Yes   (2) No   (28)

5. How often do you drink alcohol?
   (1) Never
   (2) A few drinks a year   (29)
   (3) A few drinks a month
   (4) A few drinks a week
   (5) Everyday

If you DON'T DRINK skip # 6–9; go to question 10.

6. How much do you drink when you drink?
    (1) 1 drink
    (2) 2 drinks   (30)
    (3) 3–6 drinks
    (4) more than 6 drinks
    (5) until I get "high" or drunk

7. If you drink, what do you usually drink?   (31)
    (1) wine
    (2) beer
    (3) mixed drinks
    (4) hard liquor
    (5) don't drink

8. How often do you get drunk?
    (1) Never
    (2) Once or twice a year   (32)
    (3) Once or twice a month
    (4) Once or twice a week
    (5) Several times a week
    (6) Almost every day

9. Have any of these things happened to you while you were drinking or being drunk?

	Yes	No	
a. gotten into trouble at home	1	2	(33)
b. gotten into a fight	1	2	(34)
c. had an accident or injury	1	2	(35)
d. gotten into trouble at school	1	2	(36)
e. gotten into trouble with the police	1	2	(37)

10. How many of your friends drink?
    (1) None   (38)
    (2) A few
    (3) Some
    (4) Most
    (5) All

PART II (cont'd)

11. How would your parents feel if they found out you drank alcohol? (39)
    (1) Not mad at all
    (2) Sort of mad
    (3) Really mad

PART III

Please read the following statements and decide whether each statement is true or false. If the statement is true circle "1" and if it is false circle "2".

	True	False	
1. Most people my age smoke cigarettes	1	2	(40)
2. Fewer than half the adults in this country smoke	1	2	(41)
3. Fewer people smoke now than 5 years ago	1	2	(42)
4. Cigarette smoking is becoming less socially acceptable than it once was	1	2	(43)
5. Cigarette smoke contains a poisonous gas called carbon monoxide	1	2	(44)
6. Smoking a cigarette causes your heart to beat slower	1	2	(45)
7. Smoking a cigarette will make a person more physically relaxed	1	2	(46)
8. Smoking a cigarette increases a person's blood level of carbon monoxide within a few minutes	1	2	(47)
9. Regular smokers have higher levels of carbon monoxide in their blood and lungs than nonsmokers	1	2	(48)
10. Smoking a cigarette decreases your hand steadiness almost immediately	1	2	(49)
11. Switching drinks will make you drunker than staying with the same kind of alcoholic beverage	1	2	(50)
12. Alcohol tends to pep a person up	1	2	(51)
13. Beer and wine both contain the same amount of alcohol	1	2	(52)
14. Alcohol is the most widely abused drug	1	2	(53)
15. A pregnant woman's drinking can affect the health of her baby	1	2	(54)
16. Alcohol is the cause of the majority of fatal car accidents	1	2	(55)

PART III (cont'd)

		True	False	
17.	After the effects of alcohol wear off, you are likely to be more nervous than before drinking	1	2	(56)
18.	Drinking helps people get a more restful night's sleep	1	2	(57)
19.	Most adults drink alcohol everyday	1	2	(58)
20.	People who drink the same amount of alcohol will feel and act the same	1	2	(59)

PART IV

Indicate on a scale of 1 to 5 how often you generally do the things listed below. *Circle* "1" for Never, "2" for Almost Never, "3" for Sometimes, "4" for Almost Always, and "5" for Always.

	Never	Almost Never	Sometimes	Almost Always	Always	
How often do you:						
1. Compliment your friends	1	2	3	4	5	(60)
2. Ask someone for a favor	1	2	3	4	5	(61)
3. Say "no" to someone who asks to borrow money from you	1	2	3	4	5	(62)
4. Start a conversation with someone you don't know	1	2	3	4	5	(63)
5. Tell someone you like them	1	2	3	4	5	(64)
6. Take something back to the store if it doesn't work right	1	2	3	4	5	(65)
7. Ask people to give back things that they have borrowed	1	2	3	4	5	(66)
8. Say "no" when someone asks you to do something that you don't want to do	1	2	3	4	5	(67)
9. Say "no" when someone trys to get you to smoke	1	2	3	4	5	(68)
10. Say "no" when someone trys to get you to drink	1	2	3	4	5	(69)

PART IV (cont'd)

	Never	Almost Never	Sometimes	Almost Always	Always	
11. Complain when someone gets ahead of you in line	1	2	3	4	5	(70)
12. Complain when someone gives you less change than you're supposed to get	1	2	3	4	5	(71)
13. Say "no" when someone wants to copy your homework	1	2	3	4	5	(72)
14. Ask for service in a restaurant when you are not getting it	1	2	3	4	5	(73)
15. Express an opinion even though others may disagree with you	1	2	3	4	5	(74)
16. Tell people when you think they have done something that is unfair	1	2	3	4	5	(75)
17. Ask for directions if you don't know where you are	1	2	3	4	5	(76)
18. Ask a teacher to explain something you don't understand	1	2	3	4	5	(77)
19. Ask someone out for a date	1	2	3	4	5	(78)
20. Ask a person who is annoying you in a public situation to stop	1	2	3	4	5	(79)

Card # 2 (1)
ID Code
(2–9)

PART V   Copy from first page

Below are some things that other kids have said about cigarettes and alcohol. You may agree or disagree with these statements. After reading each sentence *circle* the number under the column that comes the closest to how you feel. For example, if you strongly agree, circle the number in the column that says STRONGLY AGREE. If you disagree, but not very much, circle the number in the column that says DISAGREE.

Remember, this is not a test. We just want to know what you think.
READ EACH SENTENCE CAREFULLY BEFORE GIVING YOUR ANSWER.

	Strongly Disagree	Disagree	Neither Agree nor Disagree	Agree	Strongly Agree	
1. Cigarette smoking should not be allowed in public places	1	2	3	4	5	(10)
2. Cigarette smoke smells bad	1	2	3	4	5	(11)
3. Smoking cigarettes make you look cool	1	2	3	4	5	(12)
4. If a boy smokes cigarettes the girls will like him more	1	2	3	4	5	(13)
5. If a girl smokes cigarettes the boys will like her more	1	2	3	4	5	(14)
6. Kids who smoke have more friends	1	2	3	4	5	(15)
7. If kids smoke, it proves they're tough	1	2	3	4	5	(16)
8. Smoking cigarettes lets you have more fun	1	2	3	4	5	(17)
9. Kids who smoke cigarettes look stupid	1	2	3	4	5	(18)
10. People who smoke cigarettes are more uptight than people who don't	1	2	3	4	5	(19)
11. Kids who smoke cigarettes are show-offs	1	2	3	4	5	(20)

PART V (cont'd)

	Strongly Disagree	Disagree	Neither Agree nor Disagree	Agree	Strongly Agree	
12. Kids who smoke cigarettes are more grown-up	1	2	3	4	5	(21)
13. If kids drink alcohol, it proves they're tough	1	2	3	4	5	(22)
14. Drinking alcohol lets you have more fun	1	2	3	4	5	(23)
15. Kids who drink alcohol have more friends	1	2	3	4	5	(24)
16. People who drink alcohol are more uptight than people who don't	1	2	3	4	5	(25)
17. If a girl drinks alcohol, boys will like her more	1	2	3	4	5	(26)
18. If a boy drinks alcohol, girls will like him more	1	2	3	4	5	(27)
19. Drinking alcohol makes people act stupid	1	2	3	4	5	(28)
20. Drinking alcohol makes you look cool	1	2	3	4	5	(29)
21. Kids who drink are more grown-up	1	2	3	4	5	(30)
22. Kids who drink alcohol are show-offs	1	2	3	4	5	(31)

PART VI

Read each of these statements and indicate on a scale of 1 to 5 how much you agree or disagree with each statement. *Circle your answer.*

	Strongly Disagree	Disagree	Neither Agree nor Disagree	Agree	Strongly Agree	
1. I generally feel that I am						
a. smart	1	2	3	4	5	(32)
b. good-looking	1	2	3	4	5	(33)
c. likeable	1	2	3	4	5	(34)
d. good at sports	1	2	3	4	5	(35)
e. satisfied with myself	1	2	3	4	5	(36)
f. popular	1	2	3	4	5	(37)
g. friendly	1	2	3	4	5	(38)
h. truthful or honest	1	2	3	4	5	(39)
i. easy to get along with	1	2	3	4	5	(40)
j. a good person	1	2	3	4	5	(41)
2. I can do almost anything I put my mind to	1	2	3	4	5	(42)
3. I am generally able to do things better than most people	1	2	3	4	5	(43)
4. I am able to handle difficult situations	1	2	3	4	5	(44)
5. I feel satisfied with myself	1	2	3	4	5	(45)
6. I am a happy person	1	2	3	4	5	(46)
7. I wish I were different	1	2	3	4	5	(47)
8. It's better to do things on your own than to go along with the group	1	2	3	4	5	(48)
9. I need to be told what to do	1	2	3	4	5	(49)
10. I am easily influenced by other kids	1	2	3	4	5	(50)
11. I am able to decide things for myself	1	2	3	4	5	(51)

PART VI (cont'd)

	Strongly Disagree	Disagree	Neither Agree nor Disagree	Agree	Strongly Agree	
12. I generally get other kids to do what I want	1	2	3	4	5	(52)
13. If my friends wanted me to smoke cigarettes, I would	1	2	3	4	5	(53)
14. If someone gave me a cigarette, I would smoke it	1	2	3	4	5	(54)
15. Magazine ads and bill-boards with people smoking make me want to smoke cigarettes	1	2	3	4	5	(55)
16. I generally feel nervous when I meet new people	1	2	3	4	5	(56)
17. I generally feel confident and relaxed in social situations	1	2	3	4	5	(57)
18. I generally feel comfortable						
a. introducing myself to someone of the opposite sex	1	2	3	4	5	(58)
b. making "small talk" with someone I just met	1	2	3	4	5	(59)
c. giving compliments	1	2	3	4	5	(60)
d. receiving compliments	1	2	3	4	5	(61)
e. expressing my feelings	1	2	3	4	5	(62)
f. asking someone out for a date	1	2	3	4	5	(63)
g. starting a conversation with a stranger	1	2	3	4	5	(64)
19. When making an important decision I am usually influenced by						
a. friends	1	2	3	4	5	(65)
b. family members	1	2	3	4	5	(66)

c. teachers	1	2	3	4	5	(67)
d. newspapers, magazines, books	1	2	3	4	5	(68)
e. TV, radio, movies	1	2	3	4	5	(69)

PART VII

Please answer the following questions. *Circle your answer.* Remember, everything you say is a *SECRET*. Nobody will find out what you say.

1. Have you ever tried marijuana?   (70)

   (1) Yes   (2) No

2. Did you smoke marijuana in the last month?   (71)

   (1) Yes   (2) No

3. Did you smoke marijuana in the last week?   (72)

   (1) Yes   (2) No

4. Did you smoke marijuana yesterday?   (73)

   (1) Yes   (2) No

5. How often do you smoke marijuana?   (74)

   (1) Never

   (2) A few times a year

   (3) A few times a month

   (4) A few times a week

   (5) Everyday

6. How many of your friends smoke marijuana?   (75)

   (1) None

   (2) A few

   (3) Some

   (4) Most

   (5) All

7. How would your parents feel if they found out you smoked marijuana?   (76)

   (1) Not mad at all

   (2) Sort of mad

   (3) Really mad

PART VIII

Please read the following statements and circle "1" if it's true and "2" if it's false.

	True	False	
1. Most adults do not smoke marijuana	1	2	(10)
2. Most teenagers smoke marijuana	1	2	(11)
3. More teenagers smoke marijuana than smoke cigarettes	1	2	(12)
4. Very few junior high school students smoke marijuana	1	2	(13)
5. Peer pressure is not a factor in teenagers' decision to use marijuana	1	2	(15)
6. Smoking marijuana can cause your heart to beat faster	1	2	(17)
7. Most people are introduced to marijuana by a "pusher"	1	2	(21)
8. There is no evidence that marijuana use produces any long-term effects on the body	1	2	(23)
9. Smoking marijuana can cause a decrease in body temperature	1	2	(27)
10. Smoking marijuana can help increase our reaction time	1	2	(28)

PART IX

Answer the following questions by circling "1" for YES and "2" for NO.

	Yes	No	
1. Do you believe that you can stop yourself from catching a cold?	1	2	(30)
2. Do you believe that most problems will solve themselves if you just don't fool with them?	1	2	(31)
3. Are some kids just born lucky?	1	2	(32)
4. Most of the time do you feel that getting good grades means a great deal to you?	1	2	(33)
5. Do you believe that if somebody studies hard enough he or she can pass any subject?	1	2	(34)
6. Do you feel that most of the time it doesn't pay to try hard because things never turn out right anyway?	1	2	(35)

PART IX (cont'd)

		Yes	No	
7.	Do you feel that if things start out well in the morning that it's going to be a good day no matter what you do?	1	2	(36)
8.	Do you believe that wishing can make good things happen?	1	2	(37)
9.	Most of the time do you find it hard to change a friend's (mind) opinion?	1	2	(38)
10.	Do you think that cheering more than luck helps a team to win?	1	2	(39)
11.	Do you feel that when you do something wrong there's very little you can do to make it right?	1	2	(40)
12.	Do you believe that most kids are just born good at sports?	1	2	(41)
13.	Are most of the other kids your age stronger than you are?	1	2	(42)
14.	Do you feel that one of the best ways to handle most problems is just not to think about them?	1	2	(43)
15.	Do you feel that you have a lot of choice in deciding who your friends are?	1	2	(44)
16.	If you find a four leaf clover do you believe that it might bring you good luck?	1	2	(45)
17.	Do you often feel that whether you do your homework has much to do with what kind of grades you get?	1	2	(46)
18.	Do you feel that when a kid your age decides to hit you, there's little you can do to stop him or her?	1	2	(47)
19.	Have you ever had a good luck charm?	1	2	(48)
20.	Do you believe that whether or not people like you depends on how you act?	1	2	(49)
21.	Have you felt that when people were mean to you it was usually for no reason at all?	1	2	(50)
22.	Most of the time, do you feel that you can change what might happen tomorrow by what you do today?	1	2	(51)
23.	Do you believe that when bad things are going to happen they just are going to happen no matter what you try to do to stop them?	1	2	(52)
24.	Do you think that kids can get their own way if they just keep trying?	1	2	(53)

PART X

Read each of these statements and indicate on a scale of 1 to 5 how much you agree or disagree with each statement. *Circle your answer.*

	Strongly Disagree	Disagree	Neither Agree nor Disagree	Agree	Strongly Agree	
1. There is nothing wrong with smoking marijuana	1	2	3	4	5	(54)
2. Smoking marijuana makes you look cool	1	2	3	4	5	(55)
3. Kids who smoke marijuana have more friends	1	2	3	4	5	(56)
4. If a boy smokes marijuana, the girls will like him more	1	2	3	4	5	(57)
5. If kids smoke marijuana, it proves they are tough	1	2	3	4	5	(58)
6. Smoking marijuana lets you have more fun	1	2	3	4	5	(59)
7. Kids who smoke marijuana look stupid	1	2	3	4	5	(60)
8. People who smoke marijuana are more uptight than those who don't	1	2	3	4	5	(61)
9. Kids who smoke marijuana are more grown-up	1	2	3	4	5	(62)
10. Kids who smoke marijuana are show-offs	1	2	3	4	5	(63)
11. If a girl smokes marijuana, boys will like her more	1	2	3	4	5	(64)

PART XI

1. Which of your parents do you live with? (circle one)   (65)

    (1) Mother and Father   (2) Mother only

    (3) Father only   (4) Neither

2. How far did your father go in school? (circle one)   (66)
   (1) High School or less   (2) College
   (3) Graduate or Professional School   (4) Not sure

3. How far did your mother go in school? (circle one)   (67)
   (1) High School or less   (2) College
   (3) Graduate or Professional School   (4) Not sure

4. How many *bedrooms* are in your house?   (68)
   0   1   2   3   4   5   6   or more

5. How many cars does your family have?   (69)
   0   1   2   3   or more

6. Race: (1) Black   (2) White   (3) Hispanic   (4) Oriental   (5) Other   (70)

7. How often does your father smoke cigarettes?   (71)
   (1) Never
   (2) A few times a month
   (3) A few times a week
   (4) Everyday
   (5) Used to but quit

8. How often does your mother smoke cigarettes?   (72)
   (1) Never
   (2) A few times a month
   (3) A few times a week
   (4) Everyday
   (5) Used to but quit

9. How many of your brothers or sisters smoke cigarettes?   (73)
   (1) None
   (2) One
   (3) Two
   (4) Three or more
   (5) Have no brothers or sisters

10. How often does your father drink alcohol?   (74)
   (1) Never
   (2) A few times a year
   (3) A few times a month

PART XI (cont'd)

(4) A few times a week

(5) Everyday

11. How often does your mother drink alcohol?   (75)

   (1) Never

   (2) A few times a year

   (3) A few times a month

   (4) A few times a week

   (5) Everyday

12. How many of your brothers or sisters drink alcohol?   (76)

   (1) None

   (2) One

   (3) Two

   (4) Three or more

   (5) Have no brothers or sisters

13. Do either of your parents smoke marijuana?   (77)

   (1) No

   (2) One

   (3) Both

   (4) Not sure

14. How often does your father smoke marijuana?   (78)

   (1) Never

   (2) A few times a year

   (3) A few times a month

   (4) A few times a week

   (5) Everyday

15. How often does your mother smoke marijuana?   (79)

   (1) Never

   (2) A few times a year

   (3) A few times a month

   (4) A few times a week

   (5) Everyday

PART XI (cont'd)

16. How many of your brothers or sisters smoke marijuana?   (80)

    (1) None

    (2) One

    (3) Two

    (4) Three or more

    (5) Have no brothers or sisters

Appendix C:
Being Supportive

Being supportive gives you the opportunities to help others while learning about yourself. Below is a list of common problems and concerns. Read the list and check at least one situation that a friend of yours may have or will have in the future.

... They are in a relationship in which they are feeling a lot of pressure to engage in sexuality and they don't feel like they are ready.

... They can't seem to concentrate in school and their grades are slipping.

... Their parents want them to be home early on weekend nights, but all of their friends are permitted to stay out late.

... They feel pressure to drink beer and smoke marijuana at parties but they don't want to use drugs.

Pretend that your friend has come to you for support and wants your advice on the problem. In the space below, describe what you would say to this friend.

Dear _____

Appendix D:
About Me

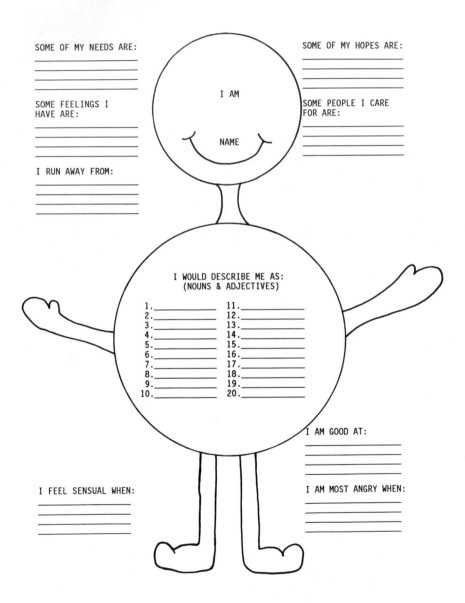

SOME OF MY NEEDS ARE:

SOME FEELINGS I
HAVE ARE:

I RUN AWAY FROM:

I AM

NAME

SOME OF MY HOPES ARE:

SOME PEOPLE I CARE
FOR ARE:

I WOULD DESCRIBE ME AS:
(NOUNS & ADJECTIVES)

1.
2.
3.
4.
5.
6.
7.
8.
9.
10.

11.
12.
13.
14.
15.
16.
17.
18.
19.
20.

I AM GOOD AT:

I FEEL SENSUAL WHEN:

I AM MOST ANGRY WHEN:

Appendix E:
Shield Against Stress

When we have skills and resources, and can use them in the face of daily challenges and problems, we have a "Shield Against Stress." Below, fill in the boxes of the shield with 6 skills or resources (i.e., "I can communicate well with my friends") that you can use to fight off stress.

YOUR SHIELD

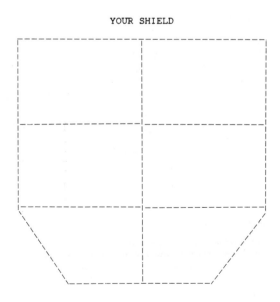

Appendix F

1.2
MEASURING MY SKILLS

Communication Skills	Doing All Right	Need to Work on This
1. Telling others what I think	_____	_____
2. Saying "no" when I want to	_____	_____
3. Listening to what other people are saying	_____	_____
4. Giving a compliment to another person	_____	_____
5. Showing others I am interested in them or getting to know them	_____	_____
6. Asking questions to get more information	_____	_____
7. Avoiding insults and putting down other people	_____	_____
8. Keeping the conversation going	_____	_____
9. Taking turns talking	_____	_____
10. Asking for a favor without demanding or threatening	_____	_____
11. Telling another person how I feel when I am angry without name calling, blaming or yelling	_____	_____
12. Being able to apologize	_____	_____
13. Following a conversation without losing interest	_____	_____

Feeling Skills	Doing All Right	Need to Work on This
1. Feeling O.K. if I say "no" to something if I think it is unreasonable	_____	_____
2. Being aware of how others are feeling	_____	_____
3. Being able to take disappointments	_____	_____
4. Being able to tell someone close how I feel about them	_____	_____
5. Being able to hug someone (mother/ father or someone close)	_____	_____
6. Being able to take name calling	_____	_____
7. Being able to accept someone not liking me	_____	_____
8. Being able to trust others	_____	_____
9. Being able to feel good about myself	_____	_____
10. Being able to enjoy other people's conversation	_____	_____
11. Being able to be alone and enjoy it	_____	_____
12. Being able to take criticism without getting angry or hurt	_____	_____
13. Being able to remain calm when another person is yelling	_____	_____

The three skills I want to work on the most:

1. _____

2. _____

3. _____

Appendix G:
Assess Your Self-Esteem

	YES	NO
· 1. Are you easily hurt by criticism?	___	___
2. Are you very shy or overly aggressive?	___	___
3. Do you try to hide your feelings from others?	___	___
4. Do you fear close relationships?	___	___
5. Do you try to blame your mistakes on others?	___	___
6. Do you find excuses for refusing to change?	___	___
7. Do you avoid new experiences?	___	___
8. Do you continually wish you could change your physical appearance?	___	___
9. Are you too modest about personal successes?	___	___
10. Are you glad when others fail?	___	___
11. Do you accept constructive criticism?	___	___
12. Are you at ease meeting new people?	___	___
13. Are you honest and open about your feelings?	___	___
14. Do you value your closest relationships?	___	___
15. Are you able to laugh at (and learn from) your own mistakes?	___	___
16. Do you notice and accept changes in yourself as they occur?	___	___
17. Do you look for and tackle new challenges?	___	___
18. Are you confident about your physical appearance?	___	___
19. Do you give yourself credit when credit is due?	___	___
20. Are you happy for others when they succeed?	___	___

Appendix H:
Building Self-Esteem

1. Who did you do something for?
2. What did you do to make this person feel better?
3. How did this person respond?
4. How did you feel?
5. What did you learn about yourself?

Appendix I:
Effective Communication Skills

Communications skills

Good ways to listen to others

1. Try to accurately listen and validate what you have heard by paraphrasing or summarizing the listener's statements.
2. Focus your attention on the speaker, maintaining eye contact.
3. Try to avoid interrupting to tell your own stories or to insert your opinion.
4. Respect and encourage the speaker by showing interest, nodding, and smiling.
5. Ask questions that indicate that you are interested in what the speaker is saying.

Good ways to express our feelings

1. Express appreciation. We often focus on what is bothering us about others while neglecting to convey the good and positive feelings we have toward them.
2. Express feelings directly. By hiding or burying our feelings within the conversation, the message can become confusing or get lost.
3. When expressing a problem, try to focus only on the targeted topic. Try to stay in the present and avoid lumping many problems together.
4. Avoiding taking up too much time when communicating. Make a point and then see if the listener understands before going on to the next point.
5. Rephrase negative accusations into direct expressions about specific behaviors (e.g., "I felt hurt when you didn't wait for me yesterday").

Appendix J:
Partners

This assignment, gives you the opportunity to reflect on the partners exercise and to imagine a more positive outcome.

Below you will find the outlines for two scripts. Fill in the first with a brief summary of what *actually* happened, and the second with what *could* have happened had good listening skills been employed.

What actually happened?

Speaker: (you can disguise the details of the problem if you want.)

Listener: (what did the listener do or say?)

Speaker: (how did the speaker respond?)

Listener:

Speaker:

What could have happened, with good listening skills

Speaker:

Listener:

Speaker:

Listener:

Speaker:

Appendix K:
Making Decisions

You and your friend are in a drug store and your friend wants you to steal a candy bar.

You and a friend are talking on the phone and you want to get off the phone.

You and a friend are at the mall and your friend sees some people she knows from another school. Your friend starts talking to them and leaves you out.

A friend tries to get you to smoke marijuana.

You are in a store and the cashier gives you the wrong change.

While at a party, a friend pulls out a bottle of alcohol and asks if you want some.

Your best friend is staying overnight. After your parents go to bed, your friend wants to go outside and mess around.

You are babysitting and the kids will not clean up their mess.

You are working with another friend on an art project but your friend will not help and wants to change the assignment to something he wants to do.

A small group of boys come up to you after school and start to pick a fight.

Appendix L:
Stop and Think

Directions: Apply the Stop & Think process to a situation in your life that needs immediate attention (e.g. a problem at home or school).

1. What is your decision or problem?
2. What is your goal?
3. What are your alternatives? (Please list them).
4. What are the pros and cons of each alternative?
5. What will you do?
6. Try it out!
7. Did it work? What happened?

Appendix M:
Substances Information Sheet

ALCOHOL

Short-term effects

Acts as a depressant, noticeable effects include drowsiness, blurred or double vision, slurred speech. Internal effects include stomach irritation and constriction of blood vessels.

Long-term effects

Alcoholism can lead to long-term physical damage including liver cirrhosis, heart disease, cell damage, shaking, sexual dysfunction, memory loss, and nutritional deficiencies.

TOBACCO

Short-term effects

Acts as a stimulant, increasing the heart rate, salivation, and leading to constriction of the blood vessels and dizziness.

Long-term effects

Nicotine addiction affects the heart, cardiovascular system, and liver. Contributes to high blood pressure, heart disease, stroke, cancer of the mouth, esophagus, lungs, larynx, and bladder. Bronchitis, teeth stains, and low birth weight in pregnant women

MARIJUANA

Short-term effects

Acts as a depressant and stimulant, increasing respiratory and heart rate, lowers body temperature, leads to visual distortion, reduces reaction time and concentration level, and can create drowsiness or alertness.

Long-term effects

Cancer of the lung and throat, short-term memory loss, male hormone abnormalities.

COCAINE

Short-term effects

Acts as a stimulant, elevating body temperature, blood pressure, heart and respiratory rate and perspiration. Can lead to euphoria, anxiety, and increased energy with subsequent depression.

Long-term effects

Addiction, hallucinations, convulsions, deterioration of nasal membranes, paranoid psychosis, and respiratory failure.

HEROIN

Short-term effects

Suppressed central nervous system reducing the feeling of pain, reduction in thirst and hunger, drowsiness, euphoria, relaxation.

Long-term effects

Addiction, use of needless may lead to acquired immune deficiency syndrome (AIDS), malnutrition, hepatitis.

LSD

Short-term effects

Elevated heart rate, blood pressure and blood sugar level. Hallucination, paranoia, reduced concentration, confusion, loss of body image.

Long-term effects

Psychosis, depression, flashbacks, chromosomal damage.

Appendix N:
No Thanks

Advertisers often use models and ideas to project positive images of drugs and drug users. Now it is your turn to be creative in response to these advertisements. Given what you know about the harmful effects of many drugs, imagine that you are an advertiser and you can respond to these messages.

Please find an advertisement for alcohol or a drug in a magazine or a newspaper and, if possible, attach it to this sheet. Please fill in the spaces below:

BRIEFLY DESCRIBE THE AD:

WHAT IS THE SUBTLE MESSAGE THAT IS BEING CONVEYED ABOUT THE DRUG?:

WHAT ADVERTISEMENT WOULD YOU CREATE TO RESPOND TO THIS AD?:

Appendix O:
A Letter to Media

This exercise encourages you to let the media know if you support or don't support their portrayal of substances. For example, given what you know about the dangers of tobacco, how do you feel about the magazine advertisements for cigarettes or television programs that depict the actors smoking? Why not let the editor or the station presidents know how you feel?

The name and address of magazine editors are usually listed in front pages. In addition, we have provided you a sample letter format and the addresses of some national television stations.

Letter Format:

> Your Name
> Street address
> City, Zip Code
> Today's Date

Addressee's Name
Address
City, State, Zip Code

Dear Mr./Ms. (Last Name),

Paragraph one Introduce yourself, where you go to school, your age, etc.

Paragraph two Tell the person why you are writing, what you saw, why you liked or didn't like it. What you would like to see stay the same or change in the future.

Thank you very much for taking the time to read this letter.

> Sincerely,

National Television Stations

CBS Entertainment
A Division of CBS, Inc.
Television City, 7800 Beverly Blvd.
Los Angeles, CA 90036
Curtis H. Philips, President

NBC Entertainment
30 Rockefeller Plaza
New York, NY 10112
John L. Lily, President

ABC Entertainment
1330 Avenue of the Americas
New York, NY 10019
John C. Severino, President

Appendix P:
Additional Role Play Situations

You are — Gary, suggests some halloween tricks and then wishes he hadn't

Situation — You invite some kids to go trick-or-treating with you. After several houses you are bored and suggest some halloween pranks. You start by soaping windows. The one boy lets the air out of some tires along the street. Everyone laughs. Then another boy suggests you all go to your teacher's house and slash his tires. Suddenly you realize that you are responsible for what is happening. How can you stop it?

Other persons — 2 friends.

You are — Jan, whose boasts threaten to ruin a girl's reputation

Situation — You boast to some older kids that you and Linda stole some makeup from the drug store. You really didn't but you want to feel important to the others. A few days later Linda asks you why you did it. The story is all over school and Linda feels her reputation is ruined. What do you do now?

Other Person — Linda, who is really a good girl.

You are — Joe, tempted to smoke marijuana cigarettes

Situation — You are at a party where everyone is smoking grass. Some close friends tell you that it's been proven that there isn't any danger and that it can't get you hooked. There doesn't seem to be any bad effects on the people you've noticed smoking. On the other hand, it is still illegal and you know that your parents strongly disapprove. Now a good friend of yours, Mel, asks you if you want to smoke: What do you say?

Other Person — Mel, a close friend who keeps pushing the idea
Your "conscience" that says "no".

You are — George, tempted to buy a "hot" tape

Situation — You've been looking around for a low-priced tape of your favorite group, but havent been able to find a good deal — until now. A guy at school has his locker filled with many tapes. You quickly realize this is stolen merchandise. Charley says, "So what, you didn't steal it." You see the tape that you've been looking for. What do you do?

Other Person — Charley, a high pressure salesman with "hot" merchandise.

Appendix Q

DRUG ALTERNATIVES

Below are listed some reasons why people use drugs. For each
reason see if you can come up with one or two possible alternatives

Motive for drug abuse	Possible alternatives
Example —	
Need for physical relaxation	Athletics ; exercise ; hiking
Now you try	
Peer pressure	
To escape boredom	
Risk ; kicks	
Peer acceptance	
To get "high"	
Depression	
To feel less inhibited	

References

Albee, G. W. (1982). Preventing psychopathology and promoting human potential. *American Psychologist, 32,* 150–161.

Aneshensel, C. S., & Huba, G. J. (1983). Depression, alcohol use and smoking over one year: A four-wave longitudinal causal model. *Journal of Abnormal Psychology, 92,* 134–150.

Bandura, A. (1969). *Principles of behavior modification.* New York: Holt, Rinehart and Winston.

Bandura, A. (1977). Self-efficacy: Toward a unifying theory of behavior change. *Psychological Review, 84,* 191–215.

Baumrind, D. (1985). Familial antecedents of adolescent drug use: A developmental perspective. In C. L. Jones & R. J. Battjes (Eds.), *Etiology of drug abuse: Implications for prevention.* Rockville, MD: National Institute on Drug Abuse, DHEW# (ADM) 56.

Beaulieu, M. A., & Jason, L. A. (in press). A drug abuse prevention program aimed at teaching problem-solving strategies. *Children and Youth Services Review.*

Berberin, R. M., Gross, C., Lovejoy, J., & Paparella, S. (1976). The effectiveness of drug education programs: A critical review. *Health Education Monographs, 4,* 337–397.

Bien, N. Z., & Bry, B H. (1983). An experimentally designed comparision of four intensities of school-based prevention programs for adolescents with adjustment problems. *Journal of Community Psychology, 8,* 110–116.

Bien, N. Z., & Bry, B. H. (1980). An experimentally designed comparison of four intensities of school-based prevention programs for adolescents with adjustment problems. *Journal of Community Psychology, 8,* 110–116.

Biglan, A., & Ary, D. V. (1985). Methodological issues in research on smoking prevention. In T. J. Glynn, C. G. Leukefeld, & J. P. Ludford (Eds.), *Prevention of adolescent drug abuse.* Rockville MD: National Institute on Drug Abuse, DHEW# (ADM) 47.

Bittikofer, J. A., & Beton, B. (1984). *Rapid drug screening in the hospital clinical laboratory,* Duke University Medical Center Publication Durham, N.C.

Blau, P. M. (1960). Structural effects. *American Sociological Review, 25,* 178–193.

Bobo, J. K. (1986). Preventing drug abuse among American Indian adolescents. In L. D. Gilchrist & S. P. Schinke (Eds.), *Preventing social and health problems through life skills training.* Seattle: University of Washington Press.

Botvin, G. J. (1985a). The Life Skills Training Program as a health promotion strategy: Theoretical issues and empirical findings. *Special Services in the Schools, 1(3),* 9–23.

Botvin, G. J. (1985b). Prevention of adolescent substance abuse through the development of personal and social competence. T. J. Glynn, C. G. Leukefeld, & J. P. Ludford (Eds.), *Prevention of adolescent drug abuse.* Rockville, MD: National Institute on Drug Abuse, DHEW (ADM) 47.

Botvin, G. J., & Wills, T. A. (1985). Personal and social skills training: Cognitive-behavioral approaches to substance abuse prevention. In C. S. Bell & R. Battjes (Eds.). *Prevention research: Deterring drug abuse among children and adolescents.* Rockville, MD: National Institute on Drug Abuse, DHEW# (ADM) 63.

Botvin, G. J., Baker, E., Resnick, N., Filazzola, A. D., & Botvin, E. M. (1984). A cognitive–behavioral approach to substance abuse prevention. *Addictive Behaviors, 9,* 137–147.

Bratter, T. (1973). Treating alienated, unmotivated drug abusing adolescents. *American Journal of Psychotherapy, 27,* 585–598.

Bronfenbrenner, U. (1979). *The ecology of human development: Experiments by nature and design.* Cambridge, Mass.: Harvard University Press.

Bry, B. H. (1985). Empirical foundations of family-based approaches to adolescent substance abuse. In T. J. Glynn, C. G. Leukefeld & J. P. Ludford (Eds.), *Prevention adolescent drug abuse,* (pp. 115–140). Rockville, MD: National Institute of Drug Abuse, DHEW# (ADM) 47.

Bry, B. H., Conboy, C., & Bisgay, K. (1986). Decreasing adolescent drug use and school failure: Long-term effects of targeted family problem-solving training. *Child and Family Behavior Therapy, 8(1),* 43–59.

Bry, B. H., McKeon, P., Pandina, R. S. (1982). Extent of drug use as a function of number of risk factors. *Journal of Abnormal Psychology, 91,* 273–279.

Campbell, D. T., & Stanley, J. C. (1966). *Experimental and quaisi experimental designs for research.* Chicago: Rand McNally.

Caplan, G. (1970). *The theory and practice of mental health consultation.* New York: Basic Books.

Cohen, C.I., & Adler, A. A. (1986). Assessing the role of social network interrelations with an inner-city population. *American Journal of Orthopsychiatry, 62(2),* 278–288.

Cohen, J. & Cohen, P. (1983). *Applied multiple regression/correlation analysis for the behavioral sciences.* Hillsdale, N. J.: Lawrence Earlbaum.

Coie, J. D., & Dodge, K. A. (1983). Continuities and changes in children's social status: A five-year longitudinal study. *Merrill-Palmer Quarterly, 29(3),* 261–283.

Cole, S. B., & Davis, D. (1978). Family therapy and drug abuse: A national survey. *Family Process, 17,* 21–29.

Coleman, J. C. (1961). *The adolescent society.* New York: The Free Press.

Cook, T., & Campbell, D. (1976). The design and conduct of quasi experiments and true design experiments in field settings. In M. Dunnette (Ed.), *Handbook of industrial and organizational psychology.* Chicago: Rand-McNally.

Cook, P. S., & Petersen, D. (1985). Individualizing adolescent drug abuse treatment. In A. S. Friedman & G. Beschner (Eds.), *Treatment services for adolescent substance abusers.* Washington, DC: U.S. Government Printing Office.

Cowen, E. L. (1977). Baby-steps toward primary prevention. *American Journal of Community Psychology, 5,* 1–22.

Cowen, E. L., Pederson, A., Babigian, H., Izzo, L. D., & Trost, M. A. (1973). Long-term follow-up of early detected vulnerable children. *Journal of Consulting and Clinical Psychology, 41,* 438–446.

Cronbach, L., & Furby, L. (1970). How should we measure change, or should we? *Psychological Bulletin, 74,* 58–80.

Danaher, G. G. (1977). Rapid smoking and self-control in the modification of smoking behavior. *Journal of Consulting and Clinical Psychology, 45,* 1068–1075.

Davis, R. M., & Jason, L. A. (1988). The distribution of free cigarettes to minors. *American Journal of Preventive Medicine, 4,* 21–26.

DeLongis, A., Coyne, J. C., Dakof, G., Folkman, S., & Lazarus, R. S. (1982). Relationship of daily hassles, uplifts, and major life events to health status. *Health Psychology, 1,* 119–136.

DeMarsh, J., & Kumpher, K. I (1985). Family-oriented interventions for the prevention of chemical dependency in children and adolescents. *Journal of Children in Contemporary Society, 17,* 274–293.

Dohrenwend, B. S., & Dohrenwend, B. P. (Eds.). (1981). *Stressful life events and their contexts.* New York: Prodist.

Downey, A. M., Butcher, A. H., Frank, G. C., Webber, L. S., Miner, M. H., & Berenson, G. S. (in press). The development and implementation of a school health promotion program for the reduction of cardiovascular risk factors in children and prevention of adult coronary heart disease: "Heart

Smart". In G. S. Berenson & B. S. Hetzel (Eds). *Reduction of cardiovascular risk factors in childhood.* The Netherlands: Elsevier Publishing Company.

Dupont, P. J., & Jason, L. A. (1984). Assertiveness training in a preventive drug education program. *Journal of Drug Education, 14,* 369–378.

Efron, D., & Rowe, B. (1987). *The strategic parenting manual.* Ontario, CA: Journal of strategic and systemic therapies.

Elliott, D. S., Huizinga, D., & Ageton, S. S. (1982). *Explaining delinquency and drug use.* Boulder: Behavioral Research Institute (Report No. 21).

Elkind, D. (1978). Understanding the young adolescent. *Adolescence, 8(49),* 127–134.

Erikson, E. H. (1959). Identity and the life cycle: Selected papers. *Psychological Issues, 1(1),* 96–136.

Evans, I. M., & Nelson, R. O. (1977). Assessment of Child Behavior problems. In A. R. Ciminero, K. S. Calhoun, H. E. Adams (Eds.), *Handbook of Behavioral Assessment.* New York: John Wiley & Sons.

Evans, R., Hansen, W. B., & Mittlemark, M. B. (1977). Increasing the validity of self-reports of smoking behavior in children. *Journal of Applied Psychology, 62,* 521–523.

Felner, R. D., Ginter, M., & Primavera, J. (1982). Primary prevention during school transitions: Social support and environmental structure. *American Journal of Community Psychology, 10(3),* 277–289.

Felner, R. D. (1988, May). *Creating supportive environments for prevention programs.* Invited paper presented at the fourth annual Illinois Department of Alcoholism and Substance Abuse Conference on Prevention. Chicago, Illinois.

Fishman, H. C., Stanton, M. D., & Rosman, B. L. (1982). Treating families of adolescent drug abusers. In M. D. Stanton & T. C. Todd (Eds.), *The family therapy of drug abuse and addiction.* New York: Guildford Press.

Flay, B. R. (1985). What we know about the social influences approach to smoking prevention: Review and recommendations. In C. S. Bell & R. J. Battjes (Eds.), *Prevention research: Deterring Drug abuse among children and adolescents.* Rockville, MD: National Institute on Drug Abuse, DHEW# (ADM) 63.

Flay, B. (1988, May). *Effective use of the mass media in prevention.* Invited paper presented at the fourth annual Illinois Department of Alcoholism and Substance Abuse Conference on Prevention. Chicago, Illinois.

Flay, B. R., & Sobel, J. L. (1983). The role of mass media in prevention adolescent substance abuse. In T. G. Glynn, C. G. Leukefeld, & J. P. Ludford (Eds.), *Preventing Adolescent Drug Abuse: Intervention Strategies.* Rockville, MD: National Institute on Drug Abuse, DHEW# (ADM) 47.

Foley, V. D. (1985). Family therapy. In R. J. Corsini (Ed.), *Current Psychotherapies* (pp. 447–490). Itasca, IL: F. E. Peacock, Inc.

Frankel, L. (1985). Structural family therapy for adolescent substance abusers and their families. In A. S. Friedman & G. Beschner (Eds.), *Treatment services for adolescent substance abusers.* Washington, DC: U.S. Government Printing Office.

French, J. F., Kaufman, J. J., & Burns, L. S. (Eds.) (1979). *Prevention Evaluation Guidelines.* Washington, DC: U.S. Government Printing Office.

Friedman, A. S. (1985a). Does drug and alcohol use lead to failure to graduate from high school? *Journal of Drug Education, 5(4),* 321–330.

Friedman, A. S. (1985b). Referral and diagnosis of adolescent substance abusers. In A. S. Friedman & G. M. Beschner (Eds.), *Treatment services for adolescent substance abusers.* Washington, DC: U.S. Government Printing Office.

Friedman, A. S., & Beschner, G. M. (Eds.). (1985). *Treatment services for adolescent substance abusers.* (Treatment Research Monograph Series, DHHS Publication N. (ADM) 85–1342.) Washington, DC: U.S. Government Printing Office.

Gambrill, E. D., & Richey, C. A. (1975). An assertion inventory for use in assessment and research. *Behavioral Therapy, 6,* 530.

Gilchrist, L. D., & Schinke, S. P. (1985a). Coping with contraception: Cognitive and behavioral methods with adolescents. *Cognitive Therapy and Research, 12,* 66–112.

Gilchrist, L. D., & Schinke, S. P. (1985b). Preventing substance abuse with children and adolescents. *Journal of Clinical and Consulting Psychology, 53,* 121–135.

Glasgow, R. E., & McCaul, K. D. (1985). Social and personal skills training programs for smoking prevention: Critique and directions for future research. In C. S. Bell & R. Batties (Eds.), *Prevention research: Deterring drug abuse among children and adolescents.* Rockville, MD: National Institute on Drug Abuse, DHEW# (ADM) 63.

Glasser, W. (1969). *Reality therapy.* New York: Harper & Row.

Glasser, W. (1985). Reality therapy. In R. J. Corsini (Ed.), *Current Psychotherapies.* Itasca, IL: F. E. Peacock, Inc.

Glidewell, J. C. (1959). The entry problem in consultation. *Journal of Social Issues, 15,* 51–59.

Gordon, N. P., & McAlister, A. L. (1982). Adolescent drinking: Issues and research. In T. J. Coates, A. C. Petersen, & C. Perry (Eds.), *Promoting adolescent health: A dialog on research and practice.* New York: Academic Press.

Haley, J. (1976). *Problem-solving therapy.* San Francisco: Harper & Row.

Haley, J. (1980). *Leaving home: The therapy of disturbed young people.* New York: McGraw Hill.

Haley, J. (1984). *Ordeal therapy.* San Francisco: Harper & Row.

Haley, N. J., Axelrod, C. M., & Tilton, K. A., (1983). Validation of self–reported smoking behavior: Biochemical analysis of cotinine and thiocyanate. *American Journal of Public Health, 73(10),* 1204–1207.

Hall, R. V., Hawkins, R. P., & Axelrod, S. (1975). Measuring and recording student behavior: A behavior analysis approach. In R. A. Weinberg and F. H. Woods (Eds.), *Observation of settings: Alternative strategies.* Reston, VA.: Council of Exceptional Children.

Hansen, W. B., Johnson, C. A., Flay, B., Graham, J. W., & Sobel, J. (in press). Affective and social influences approach to the prevention of multiple substance abuse among seventh graders. Results from project SMART. *Preventive Medicine.*

Hardy, R., & Cull, J., (1974). *Group counseling and therapy techniques.* Springfield, IL.: Charles C. Thomas.

Harris, L. S. (1985). *Problems of drug dependence, 1984.* Proceedings of the 46th annual scientific meeting, The Committee on Problems of Drug Dependence, Inc. NIDA Research Monograph 55 DHHS publication# (ADM) 85–1393.

Hartup, W. W. (1979). Peer relations and the growth of social competence. In M. W. Kent & J. E. Rolf (Eds.), *Primary prevention of psychopathology: Social competence in children.* Hanover, N.H.: University Press of New England.

Hawkins, J. D., & Lam. T. (1987). Teachers practices, social development, and delinquency. In J. D. Burchard & S. N. Burchard (Eds.), *Prevention of Drug Abuse.* Newbury Park, CA: Sage Publications.

Hawkins, J. D., Lishner, D., & Catalano, R. F. (1985). Childhood predictors and the prevention of adolescent substance abuse. In C. L. Jones & R. J. Battjes (Eds.), *Etiology of drug abuse: Implications for prevention,* Rockville, MD: National Institute on Drug Abuse, DHEW# (ADM) 56.

Hawkins, J. D., & Weiss, J. G. (1985). The social development model: An integrated approach to delinquency prevention. *Journal of Primary Prevention, 6(2),* 73–97.

Hobfoll, S. H. (in press). *The ecology of stress.* Washington, DC: Hemisphere.

Hops, H., Weissman, W., Biglan, A., Thompson, R., Faller, C., Severson, H. C. (1986). A taped situation test of cigarette refusal skills among adolescents. *Behavioral Assessment, 8,* 145–154

Howard, G. S., Schmeck, R. R., & Bray, J. H. (1979). Internal invalidity in studies employing self-report instruments: A suggested remedy. *Journal of Educational Measurement, 16(2),* 129–134.

Jason, L. A. (1977). *Research collaboration between academia and the real world.* Paper presented at the American Psychological Association, San Francisco, CA.

Jason, L. A. (1979). Preventive community interventions: Reducing school children's smoking and decreasing smoke exposure. *Professional Psychology, 10,* 744–752.

Jason, L. A., Betts, D., Kruckeberg, S., & Johnson, J. (1987, May). *A school preventive tutoring program for high-risk transfer students.* Invited paper presented at the annual meeting of the Association for Behavior Analysis, Nashville, TN.

Jason, L. A., & Bogat, G. A. (1983). Preventive behavioral interventions. In R. D. Felner, L. A. Jason, J. N. Moritsugu, & S. S. Farber (Eds.), *Preventive psychology: Theory, research, and practice*. New York: Pergamon Press.

Jason, L. A., Gruder, L., Martino, S., Flay, B. R., Warnecke, R., & Thomas, N. (1987). Worksite group meetings and the effectiveness of a televised smoking cessation interventions. *American Journal of Community Psychology, 15(1)*, 33–65.

Jason, L. A., Johnson, J., Betts, D., Smith, S., Krukenberg, S., & Cradick, M. (1987). *An evaluation of an orientation plus tutoring school based prevention program*. Manuscript submitted for publication.

Jason, L. A., Mollica, M., & Ferone, L. (1982). Evaluating an early secondary smoking prevention intervention. *Preventive Medicine, 11*, 96–102.

Jason, L. A., & Wiedenfeld, J. (1988). Selling cigarettes to minors. Manuscript in preparation.

Jessor, R., Chase, J. A., & Donovan, J. E. (1980). Psychosocial correlates of marijuana use and problem drinking in a national sample of adolescents. *American Journal of Public Health, 70*, 604–613.

Jessor, R., & Jessor, S. L. (1977). *Problem behavior and psychosocial development: A longitudinal study of youth*. New York: Academic Press.

Jessor, R., & Jessor, S. (1980). A social–psychological framework for studying drug use. In D. J. Lettieri, M. Sayers, & H. W. Pearson (1980). *Theories on drug abuse: Selected contemporary perspectives*. (NIDA Research Monograph 30, DHHS) Washington, DC: U.S. Government Printing Office.

Jessor, R. (1979). Marihauana: A review of recent psychosocial research. In R. L. Dupont, A. Goldstein, & J. O'Donnell, (Eds.), *Handbook on drug abuse*. Washington, DC: U.S. Government Printing Office.

Joffe, J. M., & Albee, G. W. (1981). Powerlessness and psychopathology. In J. M. Joffe & G. W. Albee (Eds.), *Prevention through political action and social change*. Hanover, N.H.: University Press of New England.

Johnson, C. A., & Solis, J. S. (1983). Comprehensive community programs for drug abuse prevention: Implications of the community heart disease prevention programs for future research. In T. G. Glynn, C. G. Leukefeld, & J. P. Ludford (Eds.), *Preventing Adolescent Drug Abuse: Intervention Strategies*. Rockville, MD: National Institute on Drug Abuse, DHEW# (ADM) 47.

Johnston, L. D., O'Malley, P. M., & Bachman, J. G. (1986). *Drug use among American high school students, college students, and other young adults: National trends through 1985*. Rockville, MD: National Institute on Drug Abuse, DHEW# (ADM) 86–1450.

Jones, E. E., & Segal, H. (1971). The bogus pipeline: A new paradigm for measuring affect and attitude. *Psychological Bulletin, 76*, 349–364.

Kandel, D. B. (1980). Developmental stages in adolescent drug involvement. In D. J. Lettieri, M. Sayers, & H. W. Pearson (1980). *Theories on drug abuse: Selected contemporary perspectives*. (NIDA Research Monograph 30, DHHS) Washington, DC: U.S. Government Printing Office.

Kandel, D. B. (1982). Epidemiological and psychosocial perspectives on adolescent drug use. *Journal of American Academic Clinical Psychiatry, 21(4)*, 328–347.

Kandel, D. B. (1978). Convergence in prospective longitudinal surveys of drug use in normal populations. In D. Kandel (Ed.), *Longitudinal research in drug use: Empirical findings and methodological issues*. Washington, DC: Hemisphere-John Wiley.

Kandel, D. B., Kessler, R., & Margulies, R. (1978). Antecedents of adolescent initiation into stages of drug use: A developmental analysis. In D. B. Kandel (Ed.), *Longitudinal research in drug use: Empirical findings and methodological issues*. Washington, DC: Hemisphere-Wiley.

Kazdin, A. E., & Wilson, G. T. (1978). *Evaluation of behavior therapy: Issues, evidence, and research strategies*. Cambridge, MA: Ballinger.

Kellam, S. G., & Brown, H. (1982). *Social adaptational psychological antecedents of adolescent psychopathology ten years later*. Baltimore: Johns Hopkins University.

Kelly, J. G. (1987). Seven criteria when conducting community-based prevention research: A research agenda and commentary. In J. A. Steinberg & M. M. Silverman (Eds.), *Preventing mental disorders: A research perspective.* Rockville, MD: National Institute of Mental Health, DHHS publication# (ADM) 87–1492.

Kelly, J. G., Munoz, R. F., & Snowden, L. R. (1979). Characteristics of community research projects and the implementation process. In R. F. Munoz, L. R. Snowden, & J. G. Kelly (Eds.), *Social and Psychological Research in Community Settings.* San Francisco: Jossey-Bass.

Kim, S. (1982). Feeder area approach: An impact evaluation of a prevention project on student drug abuse. *International Journal of the Addictions, 17(2),* 305–313.

Kobasa, S. C. (1979). Stressful life events, personality, and health: An inquiry into hardiness. *Journal of Personality and Social Psychology, 37,* 1–11.

Kolvin, I. (1967). Case histories and shorter communications: Aversive imagery treatment in adolescents. *Behavior Research and Therapy, 5,* 245–248.

Konopka, G. (1981). Social change, social action as prevention: The role of the professional. In J. M. Joffe & G. W. Albee (Eds.), *Prevention through political action and social change.* Hanover, NH: University Press of New England.

Kraft, T. (1970). Treatment of Drinamyl addiction. *Journal of Nervous and Mental Disorders, 150,* 138–144.

Kumpfer, K. L. (1987). Special populations: Etiology and prevention of vulnerability to chemical dependency in children of substance abusers. In B. S. Brown & A. R. Mills (Eds.), *Youth at Risk for Substance Abuse,* Rockville, MD: National Institute on Drug Abuse, DHEW (ADM) 87.

Kusnetz, S. (1985). An overview of selected adolescent substance abuse treatment programs. In A. S. Friedman & G. Beschner (Eds.), *Treatment services for adolescent substance abusers.* Washington, DC: U.S. Government Printing Office.

Lando, H. A. (1981). Effects of preparation, experimenter contact, and a maintained reduction alternative on a broad-spectrum program for eliminating smoking. *Addictive Behavior, 6,* 123–133.

LaPorte, R., Cresanta, J., & Kuller, L. (1980). The relationship of alcohol consumption to atherosclerotic heart disease. *Preventive Medicine, 9,* 22–40.

Lau, R., Kane, R., Berry, S., Ware, J., & Roy, D. (1980). Channeling health: A review of the evaluation of televised health campaigns. *Health Education Quarterly, 7(1),* 56–88.

Lazarus, R. S. (1977). Cognitive and coping processes in emotion. In A. Monat & R. S. Lazarus (Eds.), *Stress and coping: An anthology.* New York: Columbia University Press.

Lettieri, M., Sayers, M., & Pearson, H. W. (Eds.). (1980). *Theories on drug abuse: Selected contemporary perspectives.* (NIDA Research Monograph 30, DHHS) Washington, DC: U.S. Government Printing Office.

Lewis, R. A., Filsinger, E. E., Conger, R. D., & McAvoy, P. (1981). Love relationships among heroin-involved couples: Traditional self-report and behavioral assessment. In E. E. Filsinger & R. A. Lewis (Eds.), *Assessing marriage : New behavioral approaches.* Beverly Hills, CA: Sage Publishing Co.

Lewis, R. A., & McAvoy, P. (1983). Improving the quality of relationships: Therapeutic intervention with opiate abusing couples. In S. Duck (Ed.), *Personal relationships: Repairing personal relationships.* Vol. 5. New York: Academic Press.

Licarione, M. (1985). Conducting group therapy with chemically dependent adolescents. In A. S. Friedman & G. Beschner (Eds.), *Treatment services for adolescent substance abusers.* Washington, DC: U.S. Government Printing Office.

Loeber, R. (1982). The stability of antisocial and delinquent child behavior: A review. *Child Development, 53,* 1431–1446.

Loeber, R., & Dishion, T. J., (1987). Antisocial delinquent youths: Methods for their early identification. In J. T. Burchard & S. N. Burchard (Eds.), *Prevention of delinquent behavior.* Newbury Park, CA: Sage Publications.

Maccoby, N., & Alexander, J. (1979). Reducing heart disease risk using the mass media: Comparing the effects of three communities. In R. F. Munoz, L. R. Snowden, & J. G. Kelly (Eds.), *Social and Psychological Research in Community Settings,* (pp. 343–363). San Francisco: Jossey-Bass.

Marks, S. J., Darhoff, L. H., & Granick, S. (1985). Basic individual counseling for drug abusers. In A. S. Friedman & G. M. Beschner (Eds.), *Treatment services for adolescent substance abusers.* Washington, DC: U.S. Government Printing Office.

McAlister, A. L., Perry, C., & Maccoby, N. (1979). Adolescent smoking: Orset and prevention. *Pediatrics, 63,* 650–658.

Minuchin, S. (1974). *Families and family therapy.* Cambridge, MA: Harvard University Press, 1974.

Minuchin, S. (1974). *Families and family therapy.* Cambridge, MA: Harvard University Press.

Minuchin, S., Rosman, B. L., & Baker, L. (1978). *Psychosomatic families: Anoxia nervosa in context.* Cambridge, MA: Harvard University Press.

Minuchin, S., & Fishman, H. C. (1981). *Family therapy techniques.* Cambridge, MA: Harvard University Press.

Moos, R. H., Insel, P., & Humphrey, B. (1974). *Combined preliminary manual: Family, work, and group environment scales.* Pal Alto, CA: Consulting Psychologists Press, Inc.

Mulvaney, C. W. (1987). *Training in parenting skills: A program description.* St. Paul, Minn.: New Connections Programs, Inc.

Murray, D. L., O'Connell, S., Schmid, J. M., & Perry, C. L. (1987). The validity of smoking self-reports by adolescents: A reexamination of the bogus pipeline procedure. *Addictive Behaviors, (15),* 433–441.

Murray, D. M., & Perry, C. L. (1985). The prevention of adolescent drug abuse: Implications of etiological, developmental, behavioral, and environmental models. In C. LO. Jones & R. J. Battjes (Eds.), *Etiology of drug abuse: implications for prevention,* (pp. 236–256). Rockville, MD., National Institute on Drug Abuse, DHEW# (ADM) 56.

Murray, D. M., Perry, C. L., & Davis-Hearn, M. (in press). Cardiovascular risk reduction in children. *Education and Treatment of Children.*

Musto, D. F. (1973). *The American disease: Origins of narcotic control.* New Haven, CT: Yale University Press.

Nader, P. R., Sallis, J. F., Rupp, J., Atkins, C., Patterson, T., & Abramson, L. (1986). San Diego Family Project: Reaching families through the schools. *Journal of School Health, 56,* 227–231.

National Institute on Alcohol Abuse and Alcoholism. (1981). *A guidebook for planning alcohol prevention programs with Black youth* (DHHS Publication No. (ADM) 81–1055). Washington, DC: U.S. Government Printing Office.

National Institute on Drug Abuse. (1982). A chronology of growth: How parents movements evolved. *Prevention Resources, 6(1),* 11–12.

National Institute of Education. (1978). *Violent schools-safe schools: The safe school study report, 1.* Washington, DC: U.S. Government Printing Office.

Nowicki, S., & Strickland, B. R. (1973). *Journal of Consulting and Clinical Psychology, 40,* 148–154.

Olson, T., Beaulieu, M., Rhodes, J., Nicholas, J., & Jason, L. A. (1986, May). A preventive behavioral drug education program for inner-city children. Paper presented at the annual meeting of the Association for Behavior Analysis, Milwaukee, WI.

Padilla, E., Padilla, A., Morales, A., Olnedo, E., & Ramirez, R. (1979). Inhalant, marijuana, and alcohol abuse among barrio children and adolescents. *International Journal of the Addictions, 14,* 945–964.

Parkes, C. M. (1971). Psycho-social transitions: A field for study. *Journal of Social Science Medicine, 5,* 101–115.

Parsons, R. D., & Meyers, J. (1985). *Developing consultation skills.* San Francisco: Jossey-Bass.

Pearlin, L. I., & Schooler, C. (1978). The structure of coping. *Journal of Health and Social Behaviors, 19,* 2–21.

Pechacek, T. F., Murray, D. M., Luepker, R. V., Mittelmark, M. B., Johnson, C. A., & Schutz, J. M. (1984). Measurement of adolescent smoking behavior: Rationale and methods. *Journal of Behavioral Medicine, 7,* 123–138.

Pentz, M. A. (1985). Social competence skills and self-efficacy as determinants of substance use in adolescence. In S. Shiffman & T. A. Wills (Eds.), *Coping and substance use.* New York: Academic Press.

Pentz, M. A., Cormack, Dwyer, J. H., Flay, B., Hansen, W., Johnson, C. A., Mackinnon, P. P., & Wang, E. Y. I. The midwestern prevention program MPP: First year effects of a multi-community program for the prevention of drug use in adolescents. (Manuscript submitted for publication.)

Perls, F. S. (1976). Gestalt therapy verbatim: introduction. In C. Hatcher & P. Himelstein (Eds.), The handbook of Gestalt therapy. New York: Jason Aronson.

Perry, C. L., Klepp, K., & Shultz, J. M. (in press). Primary prevention of cardiovascular disease: Community-wide strategies for youth. Journal of Consulting and Clinical Psychology.

Perry, C. L., & Murray, D. M. (1985). The prevention of adolescent drug abuse: Implications from etiological, developmental, behavioral, and environmental models. Journal of Primary Prevention, 6(1), 31–52.

Piaget, J., & Inhelder, B. (1969). The psychology of the child. New York: Basic Books.

Piercy, F. P., & Frankel, B. R. (1986). Establishing appropriate parental influence in families with a drug abusing adolescent: Direct and indirect methods. Journal of Strategic and systemic Therapies, 5, 30–40.

Pinney, E. L., Schimizzi, G. F., & Johnson, N. (1979). Group psychotherapy for substance abuse patients: Development of a technique. International Journal of the Addictions, 14(3), 437–443.

Puska, P., McAlister, A., Pekkola, J., & Koskela, K. (1981). Television in health promotion: Evaluation of national programme in Finland. International Journal of Health Education, 24(4), 238–250.

Puska, P., Vartiainen, E., Pallonen, U., Salonen, J. T., Poyhia, P., Koskela, & McAlister, A. (1982). The North Karelia Youth Project: Evaluation of two years of intervention on health behavior and CVD risk factors among 13–15 year-old children. Prevention Medicine, 11, 550–570.

Resnick, H. S., & Gibbs, J. (1983). Types of peer program approaches. In Adolescent peer pressure: Theory, correlates, and program implication for drug abuse prevention. Rockville, MD: National Institute on Drug Abuse, DEW# (ADM) 86–1152.

Rhodes, J. E., & Jason, L. A. (1987). The retrospective pretest: An alternative approach to evaluating substance abuse prevention programs. Journal of Drug Education, 17(4), 345–355.

Rhodes, J. E., & Jason, L. A. (1988, March). The Operation Snowball community-based substance abuse prevention program. Invited paper presented at the First National Conference on Prevention Research Findings, Kansas City, MO.

Robins, L. N., & T. R. Przybeck (1985). Age of onset of drug use as a factor in drug and other disorders. In C. L. Jones & R. J. Battjes (Eds.), Etiology of drug abuse: Implications for prevention (pp. 75–126). Rockville, MD: National Institute on Drug Abuse, DHEW# (ADM) 56.

Rutter, M. C., & Gilder, H. (1984). Juvenile delinquency: Trends and perspectives. New York: Guilford Press.

Sameroff, A. J. (1987). Transactional risk factors and prevention. In J. A. Steinberg & M. M. Silverman (Eds.), Preventing mental disorders: A research perspective. USDHHS: Publication No. (ADM) 87–1492. pg. 74–89.

Sameroff, A. J., & Chandler, M. J. (1975). Reproductive risks and the continuum of caretaking casualty. In F. D. Horowitz, M. Hertherington, S. Scarr-Salapatek, and G. Siegel (Eds.). Review of child development research (pp. 87–244). Chicago: University of Chicago.

Schaps, E., Bartolo, R. D., Moskowitz, J., Palley, C. S., & Churgin, S. (1981). A review of 127 drug abuse prevention program evaluations. Journal of Drug Issues, Winter, 17–43.

Schinke, S. P., & Blythe, B. J. (1981). Cognitive–behavioral prevention of children's smoking. Child Behavior Therapy, 3(4), 25–42.

Schinke, S. P., & Gilchrist, L. D. (1977). Adolescent pregnancy: An interpersonal skill training approach to prevention. Social Work Health Care, 3, 159–167.

Schinke, S. P., & Gilchrist, L. D. (1984). Life skills counseling with adolescents. Baltimore: University Park Press.

Schinke, S. P., & Gilchrist, L. D. (1985). Preventing cigarette smoking with youth. Journal of Primary Prevention.

Schinke, S. P., & Gilchrist, L. D. (1983). Primary prevention of tobacco smoking. Journal of School Health, 53, 416–419.

Shapiro, A. S. (1985). Family factors and the family role in treatment for adolescent drug abuse. In A. S. Friedman & G. M. Beschner (Eds.), *Treatment services for adolescent substance abusers* (pp. 13–30). Washington, DC: U.S. Government Printing Office.

Simcha-Fagan, O., & Schwartz, J. E. (1986). Neighborhoods and delinquency: An assessment of contextual effects. *Criminology, 24(4),* 229–276.

Simkin, J. S., & Yontef, G. M. (1985). Gestalt therapy. In R. J. Corsini (Ed.), *Current psychotherapies.* Itasca, IL: F. E. Peacock, Inc.

Spitzzeri, A., & Jason, L. A. (1979). Prevention and treatment of smoking in school age children. *Journal of Drug Education, 9,* 315–326.

Spivak, G. (1983). High risk early behaviors indicating vulnerability to delinquency in the community and school. National Institute of Juvenile Justice and Delinquency Prevention, Law Enforcement Assistance Administration. Washington, D.C.: U.S. Government Printing Office.

Spivack, G., & Shure, M. (1979). *The social adjustment of young children.* San Francisco: Jossey-Bass.

Stanton, M. D., & Todd, T. C. (1982). *The family therapy of drug abuse and addiction.* New York: Guilford Press.

Stitzer, M. L., Bigelow, G. E., & McCaul, E. (1985). Behavior therapy in drug abuse treatment: Review and evaluation. In R. S. Ashery (Ed.) (1985). *Progress in the development of cost-effective treatment for drug abusers.* Research monograph 58, 31–50.

Stumphauzer, J. S. (1980). Learning to drink: Adolescents and alcohol. *Addictive Behaviors, 5,* 277–283.

Stybel, L. (1977). Psychotherapeutic options in the treatment of child and adolescent hydrocarbon inhalers. *American Journal of Psychotherapy, 31,* 525–532.

Swearington, E. M., & Cohen, L. H. (1985). Life events and psychological distress: A prospective study of young adolescents. *Developmental Psychology, 21,* 1045–1064.

Sween, J., Kyle, C. L., & Reyes, O. (1987). *Chicago public high schools: How their students' low income, reading scores, and attendance rates relate to dropout level and type of school.* Chicago: DePaul University, Chicago Area Studies Center.

Szapocznik, J., Kurtivnes, W. M., Foote, F. H., Perez-Vidal, A., & Hervis, O. (1983). Conjoint versus one-person family therapy: Some evidence for the effectiveness of conducting family therapy through one person with drug-abusing adolescents. *Journal of Consulting and Clinical Psychology, 51(6),* 889–899.

Szapocznik, J., Kurtivnes, W. M., Foote, F. H., Perez-Vidal, A., & Hervis, O. (1986). Conjoint versus-one person family therapy: Further evidence for the effectiveness of conducting family therapy through one person with drug-abusing adolescents. *Journal of Consulting and Clinical Psychology, 54(3),* 395–397.

Timer, S. G., Veroff, J., & Colten, M. E. (1985). Life stress, helplessness, and the use of alcohol and drugs to cope: An analysis of national survey data. In T. A. Wills & S. Shiffman (Eds.), *Coping and substance use.* New York: Academic Press.

Tolan, P. (in press). *Socioeconomic status, family functioning, and social stress: Correlates of antisocial and delinquent behavior in adolescents.* Manuscript submitted for publication.

Tolan, P. H., Miller, L., & Thomas, P. (in press). Perception and experience of types of social stress and self image among adolescents. *Journal of Youth Adolescence.*

Tolan, P. H., & Thomas, P. (1987). *Correlates of delinquency participation and persistence.* Manuscript submitted for publication.

Turiel, E. (1978). Social regulations and domains of social concepts. In W. Damon (Ed.), *New directions for child development: Social cognition,* (p. 1).

Vaux, A., & Ruggerio, M. (1983). Stressful life change and delinquent behavior. *American Journal of Community Psychology, 11,* 169–183.

Wells, L., & Marwell, G. *Self-esteem; Its conceptualization and measurement.* Beverly Hills: Sage Publications, 1976.

Werner, E. E., & Smith, R. S. (1982). *Vulnerable, but not invincible: A longitudinal study of resilient children and youth.* New York: McGraw-Hill.

Wills, T. A., & Shiffman, S. (1985). Coping and substance use: A conceptual framework. In S. Shiffman & T. A. Wills (Eds.), *Coping and substance use*. New York: Academic Press.

Wilson, G. T. (1985). *Behavior therapy*. In R. J. Corsini (Ed.), *Current psychotherapies* (pp. 239–278). Itasca, IL: F. E. Peacock, Inc.

Wrubel, J., Brenner, P., & Lazarus, R. S. (1981). Social competence from the perspective of stress and coping. In J. D. Wine & M. D. Smye (Eds.), *Social competence*. New York: Guilford Press.

Wunderlich, R., Lozes, J., & Lewis, J. (1974). Recidivism rates of group therapy participants and other adolescents processed by a juvenile court. *Psychotherapy: Theory, Research, and Practice, 11,* 243–245.

Yamaguchi, K., & Kandel, D. B. (1984). Patterns of drug use from adolescence to young adulthood: III. Predictors of progression. *American Journal of Public Health, 74,* 673–681.

Author Index

Subject Index

About the Authors

Jean E. Rhodes (PhD, DePaul University) is an Assistant Professor of Clinical Psychiatry at the University of Chicago Medical School. Her research interests center chiefly on substance abuse prevention, program evaluation, and behavioral medicine. Her most recent publications have appeared in the *Journal of Drug Education,* and *Children and Family Services Review.* She is a recipient of the Author J. Schmitt Academic Fellowship and the Vermont Conference on Primary Prevention Award and is an Associate Editor of *The Community Psychologist.* Presently, she is serving as the Director of Prevention Research at the Illinois Addictions Research Institute.

Leonard A. Jason (PhD, University of Rochester) is a Professor of Psychology at DePaul University. Dr. Jason is a Fellow in Division 27 of the American Psychological Association and the editor of *The Community Psychologist.* He has published over 160 articles and chapters on varied topics, including: substance abuse prevention; school-based interventions; media interventions; program evaluation; smoking cessation, and behavioral assessment. He is on the Editorial Board of the *American Journal of Community Psychology, Professional Psychology, Journal of Community Psychology, Journal of Applied Behavior Analysis, Prevention in Human Services, Behaviorists for Social Action, The Journal of Primary Prevention,* and *Special Services in the Schools,* and co-editor of the books entitled *Prevention: Toward A Multidisciplinary Approach, Preventive Psychology: Theory, Research, and Practice* and *Behavioral Community Psychology: Progress and Prospects.* Dr. Jason has received three honorable mention television media awards from the American Psychological Association and has served on review committees of the National Institute on Drug Abuse and the National Institute of Mental Health.

Psychology Practitioner Guidebooks

Editors
Arnold P. Goldstein, Syracuse University
Leonard Krasner, Stanford University & SUNY at Stony Brook
Sol L. Garfield, Washington University in St. Louis

Elizabeth B. Yost, Larry E. Beutler, M. Anne Corbishley & James R. Allender — GROUP COGNITIVE THERAPY: A Treatment Method for Depressed Older Adults

Lillie Weiss — DREAM ANALYSIS IN PSYCHOTHERAPY

Edward A. Kirby & Liam K. Grimley — UNDERSTANDING AND TREATING ATTENTION DEFICIT DISORDER

Jon Eisenson — LANGUAGE AND SPEECH DISORDERS IN CHILDREN

Eva L. Feindler & Randolph B. Ecton — ADOLESCENT ANGER CONTROL: Cognitive–Behavioral Techniques

Michael C. Roberts — PEDIATRIC PSYCHOLOGY: Psychological Interventions and Strategies for Pediatric Problems

Daniel S. Kirschenbaum, William G. Johnson & Peter M. Stalonas, Jr. — TREATING CHILDHOOD AND ADOLESCENT OBESITY

W. Stewart Agras — EATING DISORDERS: Management of Obesity, Bulimia and Anorexia Nervosa

Ian H. Gotlib & Catherine A. Colby — TREATMENT OF DEPRESSION: An Interpersonal Systems Approach

Walter B. Pryzwansky & Robert N. Wendt — PSYCHOLOGY AS A PROFESSION: Foundations of Practice

Cynthia D. Belar, William W. Deardorff & Karen E. Kelly — THE PRACTICE OF CLINICAL HEALTH PSYCHOLOGY

Paul Karoly & Mark P. Jensen — MULTIMETHOD ASSESSMENT OF CHRONIC PAIN

William L. Golden, E. Thomas Dows & Fred Friedberg — HYPNOTHERAPY: A Modern Approach

Patricia Lacks — BEHAVIORAL TREATMENT FOR PERSISTENT INSOMNIA

Arnold P. Goldstein & Harold Keller — AGGRESSIVE BEHAVIOR: Assessment and Intervention

C. Eugene Walker, Barbara L. Bonner & Keith L. Kaufman — THE PHYSICALLY AND SEXUALLY ABUSED CHILD: Evaluation and Treatment

Robert E. Becker, Richard G. Heimberg & Alan S. Bellack — SOCIAL SKILLS TRAINING TREATMENT FOR DEPRESSION

Richard F. Dangel & Richard A. Polster — TEACHING CHILD MANAGEMENT SKILLS

Albert Ellis, John F. McInerney, Raymond DiGiuseppe & Raymond Yeager — RATIONAL–EMNOTIVE THERAPY WITH ALCOHOLICS AND SUBSTANCE ABUSERS

Johnny L. Matson & Thomas H. Ollendick — ENHANCING CHILDREN'S SOCIAL SKILLS: Assessment and Training

Edward B. Blanchard, John E. Martin & Patricia M. Dubbert — NON-DRUG TREATMENTS FOR ESSENTIAL HYPERTENSION

Samuel M. Turner & Deborah C. Beidel — TREATING OBSESSIVE-COMPULSIVE DISORDER

Alice W. Pope, Susan M. McHale & W. Edward Craighead — SELF-ESTEEM ENHANCEMENT WITH CHILDREN AND ADOLESCENTS

Jean E. Rhodes & Leonard A. Jason   PREVENTING SUBSTANCE ABUSE AMONG CHILDREN AND ADOLESCENTS

Gerald D. Oster, Janice E. Caro, Daniel R. Eagen & Margaret A. Lillo — ASSESSING ADOLESCENTS